OMNIBUS EDITION

A NewTune for Flute a Day

Books 1 & 2

The useful addition of chord symbols for many of the pieces in this book will enable the teacher to provide an accompaniment on guitar or piano.

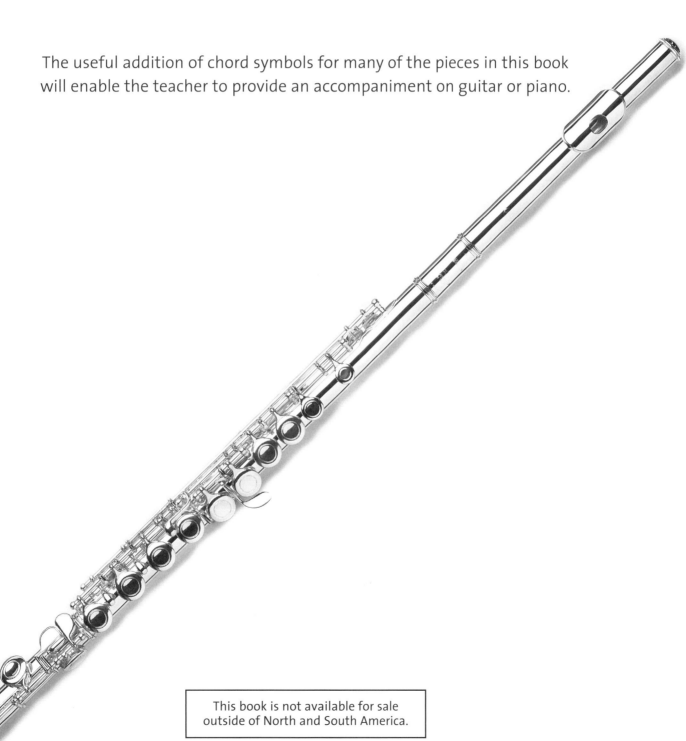

MW01040449

This book is not available for sale outside of North and South America.

Boston Music Company
part of The Music Sales Group
London/New York/Paris/Sydney/Copenhagen/Berlin/Madrid/Tokyo

Foreword

Since its appearance in the early 1930s, C. Paul Herfurth's original *A Tune A Day* series has become the most popular instrumental teaching method of all time. Countless music students have been set on their path by the clear, familiar, proven material, and the logical, sensibly-paced progression through the lessons within the book.

The teacher will find that the new books have been meticulously rewritten by experienced teachers: instrumental techniques and practices have been updated and the musical content has been completely overhauled.

The student will find clearly-presented, uncluttered material, with familiar tunes and a gentle introduction to the theoretical aspects of music. The books are now accompanied by audio CDs of examples and backing tracks to help the student develop a sense of rhythm, intonation and performance at an early stage.

As in the original books, tests are given following every five lessons. Teachers are encouraged to present these as an opportunity to ensure that the student has a good overview of the information studied up to this point.

The following extract from the foreword to the original edition remains as true today as the day it was written:

The value of learning to count aloud from the very beginning cannot be over-estimated. Only in this way can a pupil sense rhythm. Rhythm, one of the most essential elements of music, and usually conspicuous by its absence in amateur ensemble playing, is emphasized throughout.

Eventual success in mastering the instrument depends on regular and careful application to its technical demands. Daily practice should not extend beyond the limits of the player's physical endurance — the aim should be the gradual development of tone control alongside assured finger-work.

Music-making is a lifelong pleasure, and at its heart is a solid understanding of the principles of sound production and music theory. These books are designed to accompany the student on these crucial first steps: the rewards for study and practice are immediate and lasting.

Welcome to the world of music!

Published by
Boston Music Company

Exclusive Distributors:
Music Sales Corporation
257 Park Avenue South, New York, NY 10010, USA.
Music Sales Limited
14-15 Berners Street, London W1T 3LJ, England.
Music Sales Pty Limited
20 Resolution Drive, Caringbah, NSW 2229, Australia.

Your Guarantee of Quality
As publishers, we strive to produce every book to the highest commercial standards. The music has been freshly engraved and the book has been carefully designed to minimize awkward page turns and to make playing from it a real pleasure. Throughout, the printing and binding have been planned to ensure a sturdy, attractive publication which should give years of enjoyment. If your copy fails to meet our high standards, please inform us and we will gladly replace it.

Edited by David Harrison
Music processed by Paul Ewers Music Design
Original compositions and arrangements by Ned Bennett
Cover and book designed by Chloë Alexander
Photography by Matthew Ward
Model: Sasha Haworth
Printed in the United States of America
 by Vicks Lithograph and Printing Corporation
Backing tracks by Guy Dagul
CD performance by Alison Hayhurst
CD recorded, mixed and mastered by Jonas Persson and John Rose

www.musicsales.com

Contents

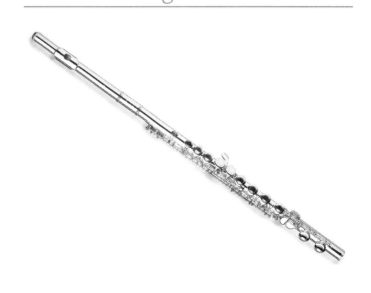

Rudiments of music

The staff

Music is written on a grid of five lines called a *staff*.
At the beginning of each staff is placed a special symbol called a *clef* to describe the approximate range of the instrument for which the music is written.

This example shows a *treble clef*, generally used for melody instruments.

The staff is divided into equal sections of time, called *bars* or *measures*, by *barlines*.

Note values

Different symbols are used to show the time value of *notes*, and each *note value* has an equivalent symbol for a rest, representing silence.

The **eighth note**, often used to signify a half beat, is written with a solid head and a stem with a tail. The eighth-note rest is also shown.

The **quarter note**, often used to signify one beat, is written with a solid head and a stem. The quarter-note rest is also shown.

The **half note** is worth two quarter notes. It is written with a hollow head and a stem. The half-note rest is placed on the middle line.

The **whole note** is worth two half notes. It is written with a hollow head. The whole-note rest hangs from the fourth line.

Other note values

Note values can be increased by half by adding a dot after the note head. Here a half note and quarter note are together worth a *dotted* half note.

Grouping eighth notes

Where two or more eighth notes follow each other, they can be joined by a *beam* from stem to stem.

Time signatures

The number of beats in a bar is determined by the *time signature*, a pair of numbers placed after the clef.
The upper number shows how many beats each bar contains, while the lower number indicates what kind of note value
is used to represent a single beat. This lower number is a fraction of a whole note, so that 4 represents quarter notes
and 8 represents eighth notes.

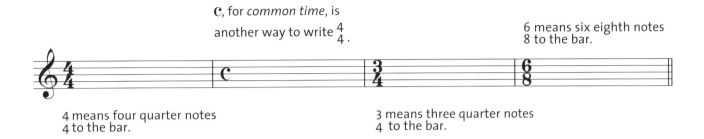

C, for *common time*, is
another way to write 4/4.

6 means six eighth notes
8 to the bar.

4 means four quarter notes
4 to the bar.

3 means three quarter notes
4 to the bar.

Note names

Notes are named after the first seven letters of the alphabet and are written on lines or spaces on the staff,
according to pitch.

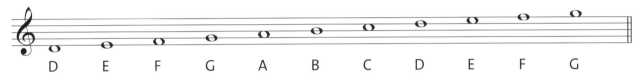

D E F G A B C D E F G

Accidentals

The pitch of a note can be altered up or down a half step (or *semitone*) by the use of sharp and flat symbols.
These temporary pitch changes are known as *accidentals*.

The *sharp* (♯) raises the pitch of a note.

The *natural* (♮) returns the note to its original pitch.

The *flat* (♭) lowers the pitch of a note.

Ledger lines

Ledger lines are used to extend the range of the staff for low or high notes.

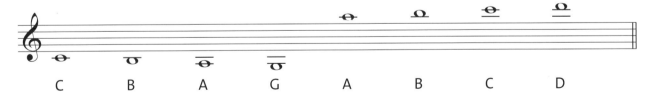

C B A G A B C D

Barlines

Various different types of barlines are used:

Double barlines divide one section of music from another.

Final barlines show the end of a piece of music.

Repeat marks show a section to be repeated.

5

Before you play:

The flute and accessories Your complete flute outfit should include the following:

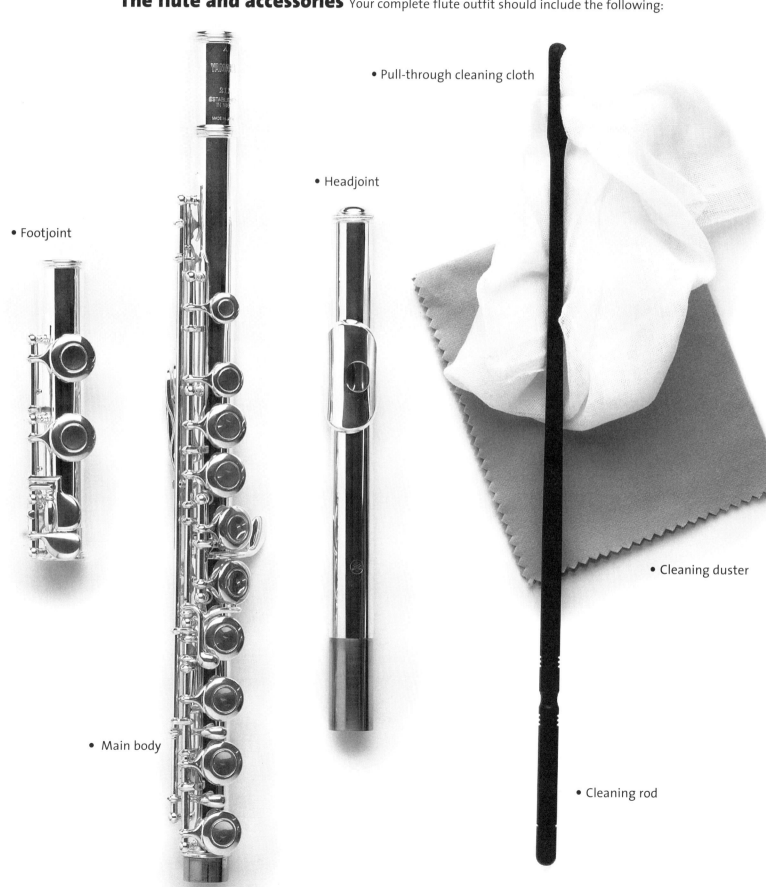

• Pull-through cleaning cloth

• Headjoint

• Footjoint

• Main body

• Cleaning duster

• Cleaning rod

Setting-up routine

1. Use a twisting action to push the footjoint gently onto the main body of the flute. Align the rod of the footjoint with the keys on the main body.

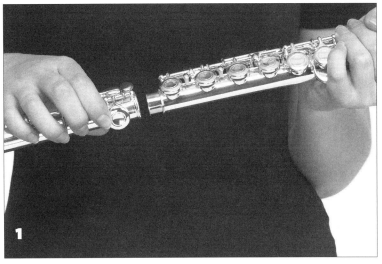

2. Again with a twisting action push the headjoint into the main body. Align the center of the lip hole with the center of the keys.

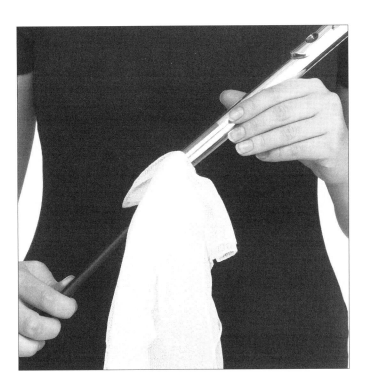

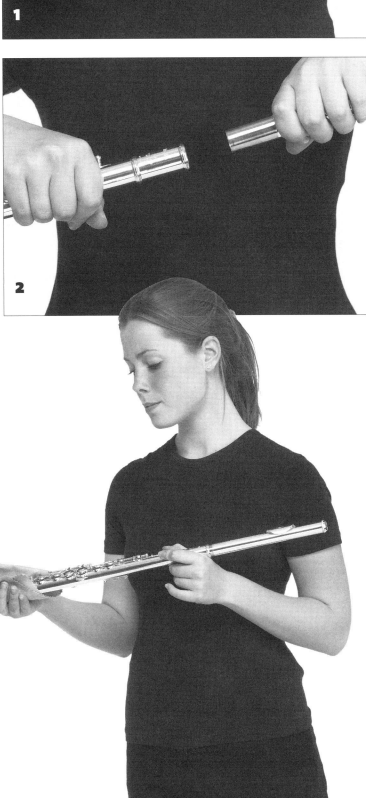

Important

Always dry your flute thoroughly after playing using the cleaning rod to push the cloth down inside the instrument. Make sure the rod is completely covered to prevent the risk of scratching the inside of the flute.

Don't keep the damp cloth in the case with your flute.
Never use polish to clean the outside of the flute; a soft, clean cloth is ideal.

Lesson 1

goals:

1. Breathing using the diaphragm
2. Formation of the mouth shape (embouchure)
3. Tonguing
4. Holding the flute
5. The notes B, A and G
6. Counting while playing; whole notes, half notes, and quarter notes

Breathing

A relaxed, controlled posture is essential for comfort and correct breathing.

When breathing in and out, always use your diaphragm. This is a large membrane underneath your rib cage which causes your stomach to go *out* when breathing in and to go *in* when breathing out.

You will be able to control your breathing far more effectively using your diaphragm than if you were to breathe with the *intercostal* muscles high up in your chest.

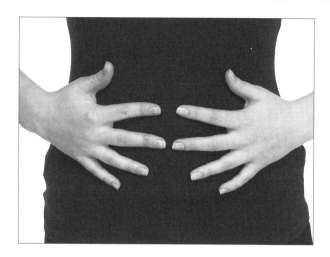

Exercise 1:

Breathe in counting four beats, then breathe out counting 4 and so on, always using the diaphragm and maintaining a steady flow of air.

In, 2, 3, 4,   Out, 2, 3, 4,   In...

Place one hand on your stomach to check whether it is going out as you breathe in then in when you breathe out.

Tonguing and embouchure

To produce your first sound, it is easiest to work with just the headjoint, so remove it from the rest of the flute. Say the word *too* and then say it again without engaging your vocal chords. Notice how your tongue acts as a valve that blocks the air flow until the desired moment.

Hold the head joint in front of your mouth with the open end to the right, and the mouth hole central to your lips. While keeping the mouth hole level, feel for the near edge of the hole with the bottom edge of your bottom lip. Press the headjoint on firmly. Your bottom lip should cover just a third of the hole.

Exercise 2: your first notes

Breathe in while setting the embouchure.

Play these four notes, tonguing each one and counting steadily throughout.

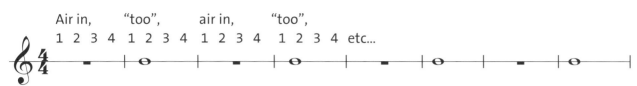

Air in,   "too",   air in,   "too",
1 2 3 4 1 2 3 4 1 2 3 4   1 2 3 4 etc...

Make sure the cheeks remain taught: don't puff them out.

Now reassemble the flute, hold it up without pressing any of the keys and repeat exercise 2.

Holding the flute

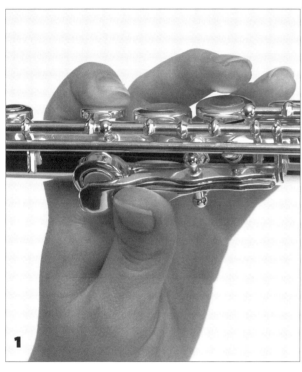

1

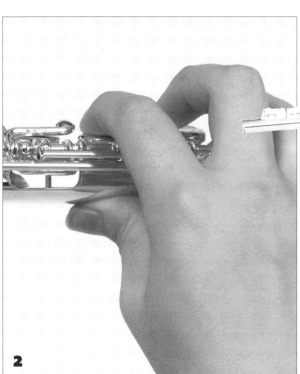

2

Position the top joint of your left thumb over the long *paddle-shaped* key at the back.

The flute rests on the lowest section of your index finger. Curl it around to the front, hugging the body of the flute.

Cover the keys as shown in picture 1.

Now place the tip of your right thumb underneath the flute beneath the third key from the bottom end of the main body.

Curl your fingers over the top and cover the lowest three circular keys of the main body as shown in picture 2.

Now push down the top key on the footjoint with your little finger.

Lesson 1

The notes B, A and G

B

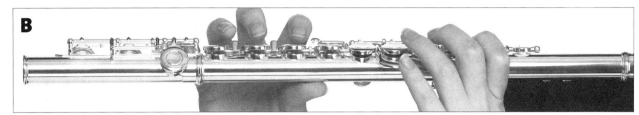

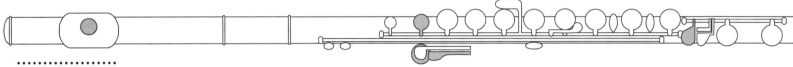

NOTE
Throughout this book, the fingering diagrams are shown from the point of view of the player.

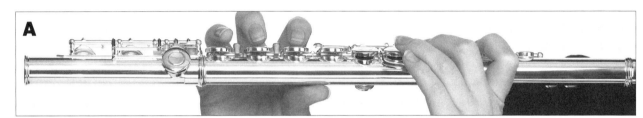

A

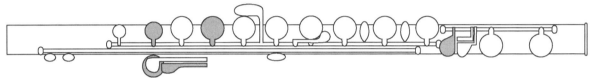

G

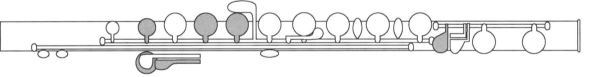

Exercise 3:

Breathe before the beginning of this exercise and in the rests.

Don't forget to tongue each note. A four-beat note is called a **whole note**.

Exercise 4:

Each of the notes and rests here are **half notes,** worth two beats.

Exercise 5:

These notes and rests are all **quarter notes,** worth one beat each. Breathe in quickly during quarter-note rests.

Pieces for Lesson 1

Valley Song

CD1 3

Going Cuckoo

CD1 4

Au Clair de la Lune

CD1 5-6

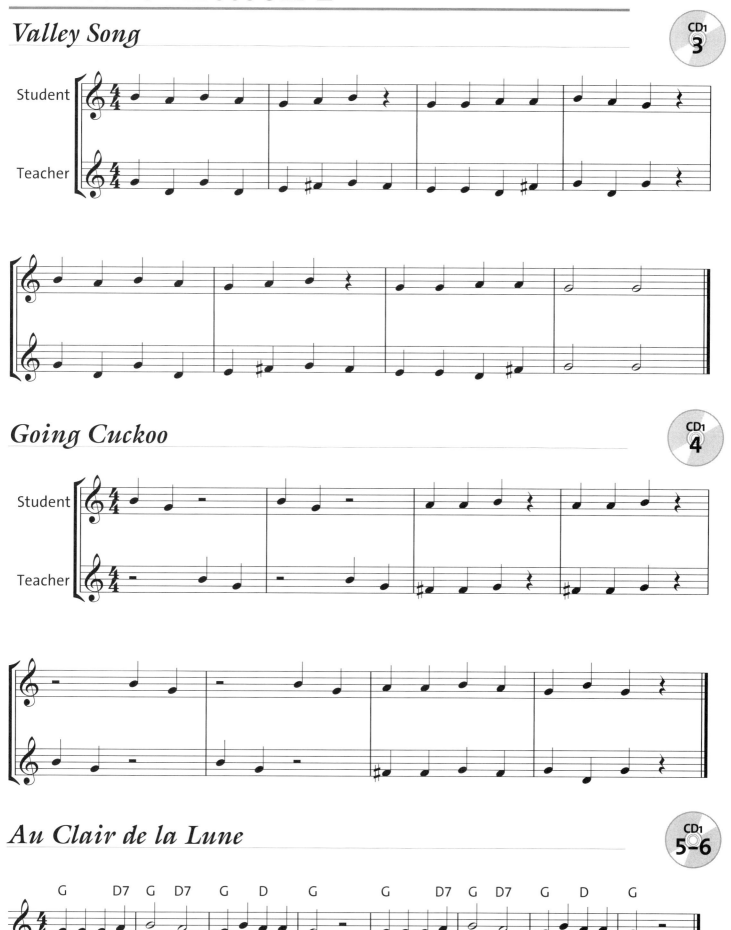

Lesson 2 — goals:

1. **The note C**
2. **Open throat breathing**
3. **Dotted half notes**
4. **Three beats in a bar**

The note C

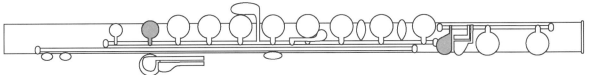

> ### OPENING YOUR THROAT
>
> Blow on the back of your hand. You will feel the air is cold.
> Now try again, pretending that you are steaming up a window.
> This time the air on the back of your hand should feel warm because you have just breathed out with your throat open. You should keep your throat open at all times when playing as it will improve your tone.

Exercise 1:

Stand with a relaxed posture, take a good deep breath and play the note with an open throat, using the diaphragm to control the air flow.

The symbol above this note is called a **pause** (or *fermata*). It means you should hold the note for longer than its actual value of four beats. Hold this one for as long as you can. Play with an **open throat**.

Long notes like this one should be the first thing you practice every day.

Exercise 2:

Play these notes in tempo with an open throat. The little commas are *breath marks*.

Take a very quick breath here without disrupting the 4-beat count.

Exercise 3:

The coordination of your fingers and your tongue is called *articulation*.

It is very important to develop this so all notes sound clean and precise.

Don't be satisfied with any untidiness!

Dotted notes

A dot placed to the right of a note multiplies its duration (value) by one and a half.

This means that a half note with a dot would increase in duration from two beats to three (2+1=3).

Count: 1 2 3 4   1 2 3 4

Exercise 4:

Count carefully as you play these notes. Remember the open throat.

Time signatures

So far all the exercises and pieces have had a **time signature** of four beats to every bar:

1 , 2 , 3 , 4 , **1** , 2 , 3 , 4 , **1** , 2 , 3 , 4 etc.

Many pieces, however, contain three beats per bar.

This means that the count in your head will be **1** , 2 , 3 , **1** , 2 , 3 , **1** , 2 , 3 etc.

A waltz is a dance that uses this time signature.

Exercise 5:

Count three beats per bar, as shown by the top number of the time signature, and make sure you don't get confused between notes in spaces (A and C) and notes on lines (G and B).

Count: 1 2 3   1 2 3   1 2 3

THINK!

Are you still relaxed when you play? Remember to keep your shoulders down and breathe using your diaphragm.

Check that your bottom lip is in the correct position when you play, and that your right little finger is always pushing its key down.

Pieces for Lesson 2

CD1 **7-8**

Back To Bed

CD1 **9**

Grumpy Graham

CD1 **10**

Medieval Dance

CD1 **11**

Barcarolle

Offenbach

goals:

1. **The notes F and B flat (B♭)**
2. **Tones and semitones**
3. **Tied notes**
4. **The key of F major**

The notes F and B♭

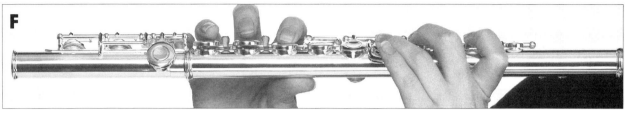

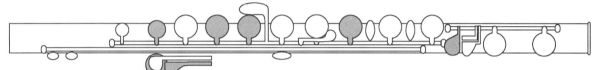

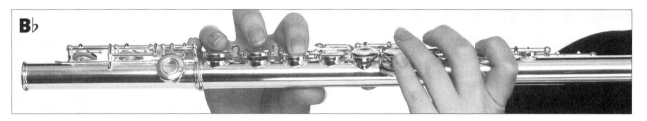

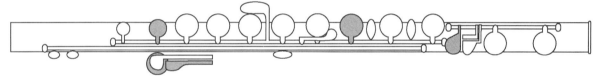

Exercise 1:

Play this one a few times, holding the note for as long as is comfortable.

Exercise 2: tones and semitones

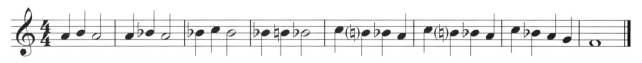

The difference in pitch between A and B is called a tone. A to B♭ is only a semitone, and B♭ to B is also a semitone. A semitone is the smallest interval that can be played on most instruments.

Exercise 3:

Play this one many times to ensure that your tongue, fingers and thumb (if needed) all move together.

Exercise 4:

Don't get confused between F, A, and C, which all look a bit similar.

Lesson 3

Ties and tied notes

Two notes of the same pitch can be joined together to make a longer note by *tying* them together.
A curved line is drawn from one to the other to show this. The note is then held for the *combined value*
of the two notes. This is usually needed if a note needs to carry into the next bar.
Here are some examples:

is held for **3** beats   is held for **6** beats

Exercise 5:

Count very carefully here.

Count: **1   2   3   4   1   2...**

Different keys

If you try to sing a simple tune such as *The Star Spangled Banner*, you may find early on that you can't reach
the high notes without really straining. The solution is to start the piece a little lower. This time, you may be
able to sing the high notes perfectly. You are now singing the piece in a different *key*.

There are many different keys in music, each of which needs its own set of notes.
The key of C major is easy as it requires only natural notes. The key of F major requires all Bs to be B♭.
The key of a piece is shown by a *key signature*.

C major

F major

Notice that exercises 3 and 5 require B♭ instead of B, and that they begin and end on the note F.
They are all in the key of F major.

Exercise 6: reading music with a key signature

You must play all Bs as B♭s.

Exercise 7: comparing music in two different keys

The first is in G major (don't worry about the the sharp symbol in the key signature, you won't need it).
The second is in F major.

Pieces for Lesson 3

Jingle Bells

Largo (from the New World Symphony)   Dvořák

Lightly Row

Knight Time

Lesson 4

goals:

1. **The note D in the middle register**
2. **Dynamics (loud and soft)**
3. **Slurred notes**

The note D

 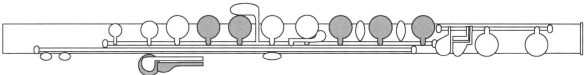

Try to make a slightly smaller hole between your lips and push your bottom lip forward a fraction. You must also remove your right little finger.

Exercise 1:

Hold each note for a full breath. Breathe between each one.

Exercise 2: fiddling fingers

Practice this very slowly to begin with, and build up the speed until all the fingerings become automatic.

Exercise 3: moving by step and by *leap* in two keys

F major   G major

Dynamics

Notes and rhythms are two of the elements of music, but without expression, music can be lifeless and mechanical. One of the obvious ways of introducing *color* into music is to play sections of pieces or phrases at different levels of loudness.

f stands for the word *forte* and means loud.   *p* stands for the word *piano* and means quiet.

Exercise 4:

Play these notes according to the dynamic displayed underneath.
Use your diaphragm to increase the airflow for the loud notes, and decrease the airflow for the quiet ones.

Slurs

In all the pieces and exercises so far you have tongued every note, that is, you have started each note with a *t* as in *too*. This can make the music sound a bit disjointed, and spoils the flow of gentle pieces such as *Barcarolle* in lesson 2.

Music is made smoother by slurring notes together. This means you should only tongue the first note of the slur. All other notes included in the slur are played by just changing the fingering.
Slurs are shown by lines which look like ties, but the notes will be of different pitches.

Exercise 5: slurred pairs

Only tongue the first of each pair of notes, but keep the air flowing as you play the second.

Exercise 6:

You must slur three notes at a time here. The steady **1**, 2, 3 count is unaffected by slurs.

Exercise 7:

Try *Barcarolle* again with slurs and with the dynamic shown. It should sound much more like a lullaby.

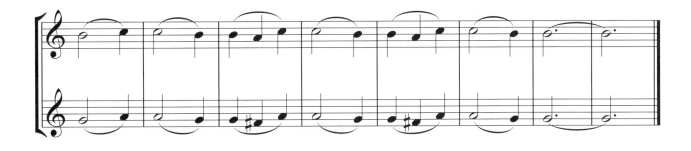

Pieces for Lesson 4

CD1 19–20
When The Saints Go Marching In

CD1 21–22
Joshua Fought The Battle Of Jericho

Spiritual

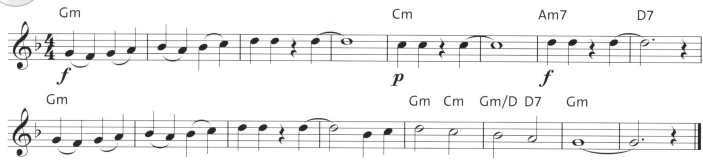

CD1 23–24
Coventry Carol (adapted)

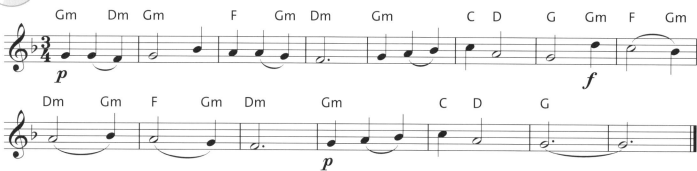

Canon For Two

The second player starts one bar behind the first player.

goals:

1. **The note E, and F in the middle register**
2. **Octaves**
3. **The F major scale**
4. **Repeat signs**

The note E, and F in the middle register

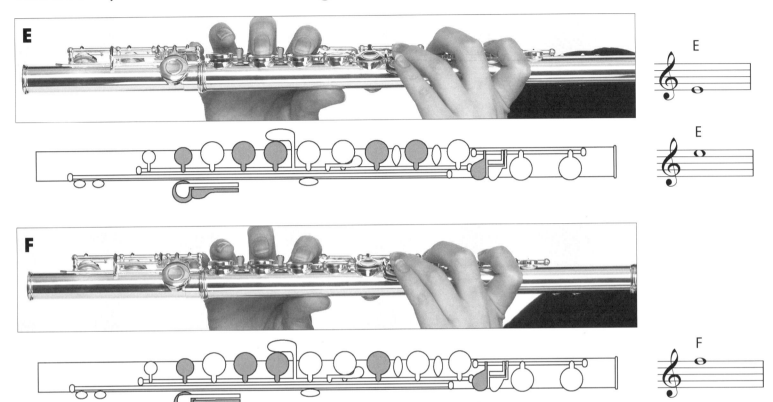

Exercise 1:

Compare the sounds of low E with the *higher* E and low F with the *higher* F.

Exercise 2:

Awkward finger movements need lots of practice.

Try this many times every day, both tongued and slurred as shown.

The thick bar-lines with two dots tell you to **repeat** the music between them, in other words play *twice*.

Don't forget: your little finger is off for the D and back on for the E and F.

Exercise 3: the F major scale

This is the set of notes in the key of F major, ascending and descending by step.

21

Pieces for Lesson 5

Barcarolle

Offenbach

A new key for this piece.

Although you could play the lower part, the upper part would provide much better practice!

Student

Teacher

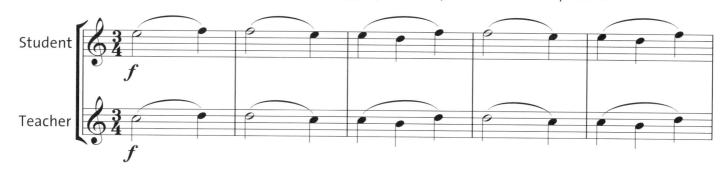

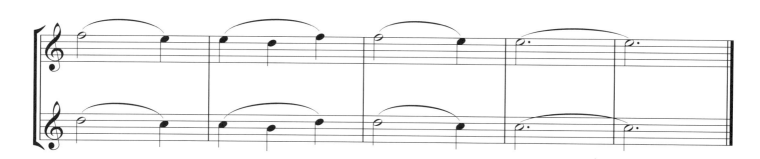

Abide With Me

Monk

Student

Teacher

Pieces for Lesson 5

Juggling

My Favorite Waltz

Pieces for Lesson 5

Minuet

THINK!

Don't be lazy with your tonguing –
proper articulation is essential
for a clear sound.

test:

for Lessons 1 to 5

1. Note duration

On the staff below, draw notes of the indicated duration:

4 beats   2 beats   1 beat   3 beats

(4)

2. Rests

On the staff below, draw rests of the indicated duration:

4 beats   2 beats   1 beat   3 beats

(4)

3. Notes

On the staff below, draw the following notes as half notes:

G, **B**, **low E**, **C**, **high F**, **D** and **B♭**

(8)

4. Scales

Write out the F major scale including the key signature.

(2)

5. Bars

Draw barlines on this staff where they are needed.

(7)

Total (25)

Lesson 6

goals:

1. **The note F sharp (F♯)**
2. **Octaves**

The note F♯

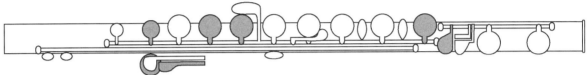

The sharp symbol (♯) raises the note to which it applies by a semitone.

This means that **F♯** is a semitone *above* **F** and a semitone *below* **G**.

Exercise 1:

Listen to how close F♯ and G sound

Exercise 2:

There is a tricky fingering change from E to F♯, and from D to F♯. This exercise needs to be practiced frequently.

(Once a note is sharped, it remains so throughout the bar unless a natural sign is employed.)

Exercise 3: octave practice

Remember to adjust the embouchure.

Pieces for Lesson 6

Steal Away

Spiritual

Sea Song

Finger Blues

Lesson 7 goals:

1. **The notes G (middle register) and low D**
2. **Common time**
3. **G major scale**

The notes G (middle register) and low D

G

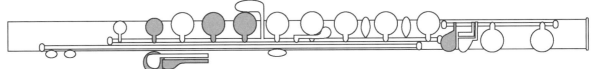

D

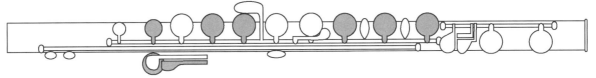

Exercise 1:

Practice makes perfect. Low notes can be a little tricky to play at first, but perseverance will be rewarded with a good, strong tone.

Work your way down to a low D, keeping your breath even.

Make sure your little finger stays firmly down until the moment you play the D.

Exercise 2:

Make sure you are breathing from your diaphragm for complete breath control, and experiment with your embouchure until these low notes come easily. And most important of all: relax!

Low notes can be hard to play with a strong tone. Ensure that your throat is open.

Imagine the shape of your throat when you steam up a window.

The large **c** at the beginning of this staff is shorthand for **common time,** which is the same as $\frac{4}{4}$.

Exercise 3:

G major scale and *arpeggio*.

28

Pieces for Lesson 7

O Come All Ye Faithful

CD1 38-39

Skye Boat Song

Scottish traditional

CD1 40-41

Repeat the section within the repeat signs, then go back to the beginning and play until the sign *Fine* (Italian for "end").

Scarborough Fair

English traditional

CD1 42

You could play the top part or the bottom part. If you feel ambitious, learn both!

goals:

1. **The note C sharp (C♯)**
2. **Eighth notes**

3. **D major scale**
4. **Tempo and character markings**

The note C♯

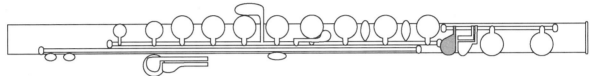

Exercise 1:

A tricky fingering change from C♯ to D.

Eighth notes

Single eighth notes and an eighth-note rest

So far you have studied and played notes that last for four beats (whole note), two beats (half note), and one beat (quarter note). You have also learned how to increase note durations by tying notes together or by adding a dot to a half note (for a three-beat note).

Eighths in pairs (worth one quarter per pair)

Eighth notes are notes which last for *half* the length of a quarter notes and should therefore be played *twice* as fast.

Exercise 2: *double or quit!*

Keep the beat steady and don't start too quickly.

Eighth notes as a group (a half note's worth)

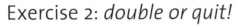

Count: 1 2 3 4 1 2 3 4 1 2 3 4 1 & 2 & 3 & 4 & 1 2 3 4

Exercise 3: three beats per bar

Sight-reading (playing music that you haven't seen before) is an important skill for a musician.

Count: 1 2 3 1 2 3 1 & 2 & 3 & 1 2 3

Exercise 4: the scale of D major

Play this both slurred and tongued (as shown by the dotted slur lines).

30

Pieces for Lesson 8

Some short melodies for practice at playing eighth notes.

Yankee Doodle

This piece has only two beats per bar, and notice the tempo (speed) marking above the beginning of the piece.

Can Can

Offenbach

Nessun Dorma

Puccini

From *The Magic Flute*

Mozart

Swing Low, Sweet Chariot

Spiritual

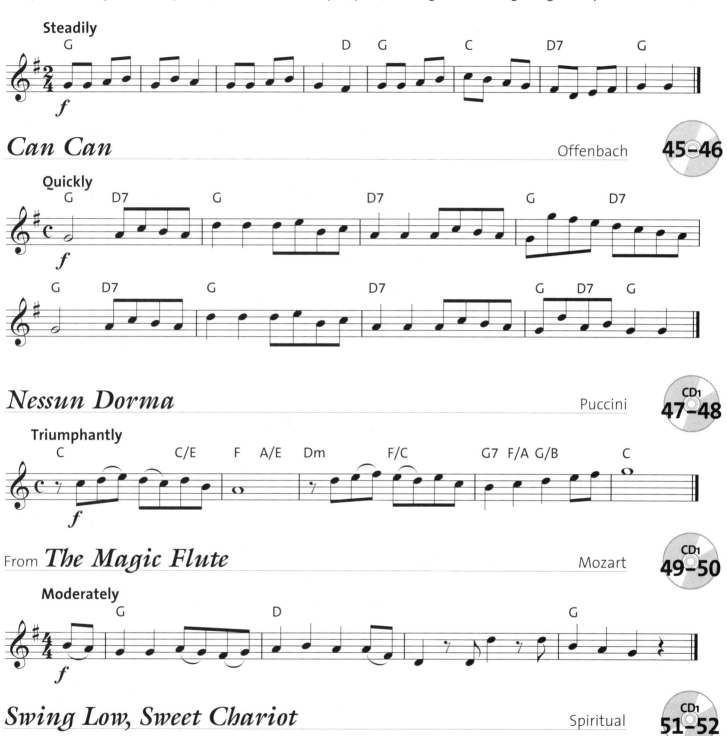

Lesson 9 goals:

1. **The note A in the middle register**
2. **Dotted quarter notes**

The note A in the middle register

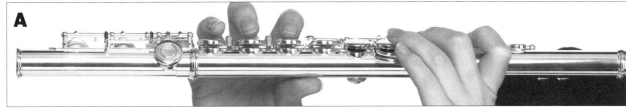

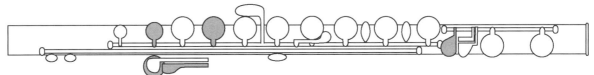

Exercise 1:

Play each note for as long as you can. Every time you practice you should start with long notes!

Exercise 2:

This is to help your control over octave leaps. Always aim for a clear sound in both the lower and middle register. Remember to adjust your embouchure rather than blowing harder. Play this slowly.

Dotted quarter notes

Dotted notes are often used instead of tying notes together: the fewer symbols there are on the page, the easier the music is to read.

As long ago as lesson 2 you discovered that a dot placed to the right of a half note increased its value from two beats to three. You could say that the dot *multiplies* its length by one and a half.

The same dot can be used to increase a quarter note's length from one beat to one and a half beats. In other words, instead of being the same length as two eighth notes tied together, its value is raised to three eighth notes.

Exercise 3:

Play this slowly so that you can count each eighth note. Learn to recognize the rhythms as you recognize words without really having to read them.

Count: 1 & 2 & 3 & 4 & 1 & 2 & 3 & 4 & 1...

32

Exercise 4:

Play this exercise a few times, increasing the speed a little each time.

In time you should feel the rhythm and rely less on having to count each eighth note.

Exercise 5:

Because this type of rhythm is very common but a little tricky, here is another exercise.

This time there are three beats to a bar.

Pieces for Lesson 9

Auld Lang Syne

Sometimes a piece of music doesn't begin with a whole bar.

This piece begins with a single beat representing the last beat of a bar. This short bar (called an *upbeat* or *anacrusis*) is balanced by another short bar at the end. The two short bars add up to a whole bar.

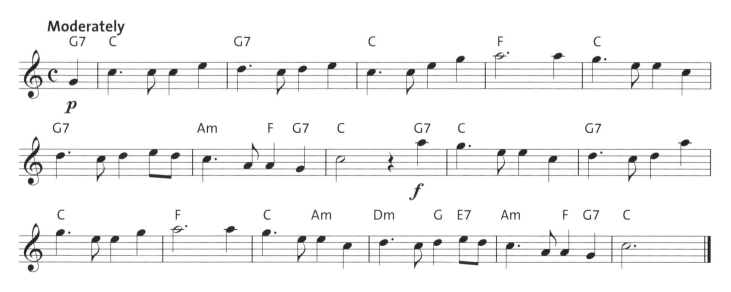

Pieces for Lesson 9

Allegro from *Spring* (adapted)

Vivaldi

Allegro is the Italian word for "quick" and is very commonly seen as a tempo marking in music.

The top line here is the main tune, but you could also learn the bottom line for duet playing.

THINK!

Are you practicing properly?

Always start with long notes, making sure you are using your diaphragm and open throat. Stay relaxed when you play. Practice your exercises every day to build up embouchure strength. Don't be satisfied if a piece is nearly right.

It needs to be completely right before you should move on.

goals:

1. **Tone practice**
2. **More dynamics**

Practicing long notes *every day* is essential for developing a better sound.
Not only are you training your embouchure, diaphragm and throat, you are also building up vital muscle groups that improve your stamina and projection.

Exercise 1:

Use a full breath for each note. Rest between each one.

Exercise 2:

A clear tone in the middle register is hard to achieve. Aim to reduce the breath noise on all these notes.

Exercise 3:

Listen carefully to make sure that the lower register note is in tune with the middle register one,
and that they are at the same volume.

More dynamics

Only *p* and *f* have been introduced so far. These tell you to play either quietly or loudly. However, in between these extremes you could play *moderately quiet* or *moderately loud*. These are shown by the markings *mp* and *mf*. The *m* is short for *mezzo*, which is the Italian word for "half."

Exercise 4:

Play these notes with the dynamics indicated.

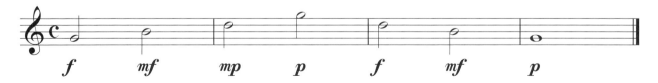

Pieces for Lesson 10

Hark! The Herald Angels Sing

Dixie

Emmett

From **Symphony No.9** (play either part)

Beethoven

test:
for Lessons 6 to 10

1. Note duration

On the staff below, draw notes of the indicated duration:

| | 2 beats' worth | dotted | a note that lasts |
| 1 eighth note | of eighth notes | quarter note | for 5 eighth notes |

(8)

2. Scale

On the staff below, draw the G major scale including the correct key signature:

(4)

3. Notes

On the staff below draw the following notes as quarter notes:

F♯, A, D (all middle register), and **low E**

(4)

4. Dynamics

What are the Italian words for:

Moderately loud _____

Moderately quiet _____

(4)

5. Naming ceremony

Identify all the items indicated by arrows.

Allegro

p

(5)

Total **(25)**

Lesson 11 goals:

1. The notes E flat (E♭) and B flat (B♭)
2. The key of B♭ major

The notes E♭ and B♭

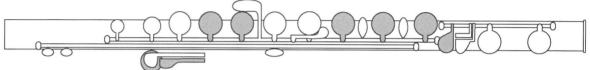

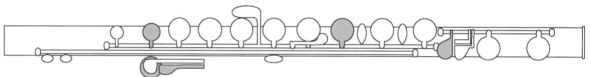

Exercise 1:

Make sure you change all the necessary fingers.

Remember to take your left index finger off for D and E♭ in the middle register.

Exercise 2: "the worm of misery"

In this exercise all notes are a semitone apart. This one will need a good deal of practice.

Exercise 3:

The scale and arpeggio of B♭ major. Remember what the key signature tells you.

Pieces for Lesson 11

Frère Jacques

French traditional

Up to four people can play this as a round. Begin when the previous instrument gets to the star in the third bar.

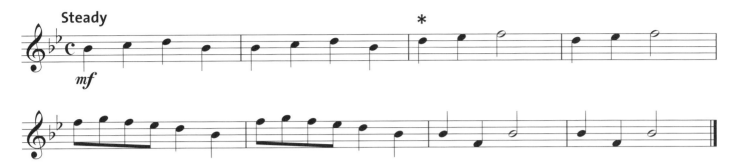

Romance No.1

Beethoven

Maintain a calm and steady tone throughout.

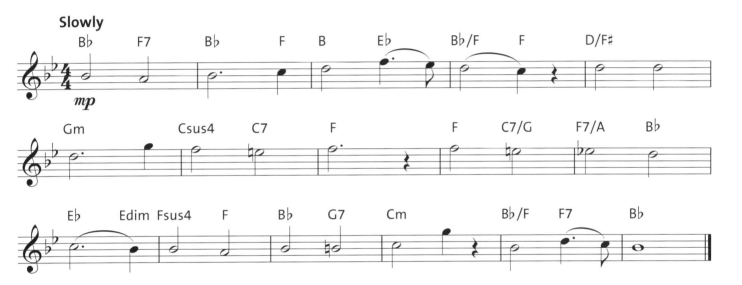

Can Can

Offenbach

Compare this version in F major with the one in G major in lesson 8.

goals:

1. **The notes B and C in the middle register**
2. **D.S. al Fine**

You might find that these high notes sound a little out of tune when you first play them. Keep a firm embouchure to ensure a steady tone and correct tuning.

The notes B and C in the middle register

B

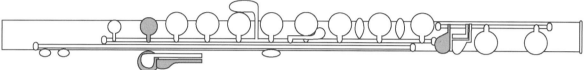

C

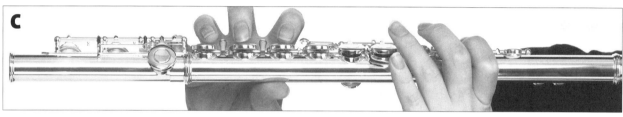

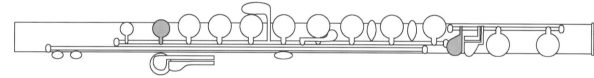

Exercise 1: long notes in the middle register

Exercise 2: octave slurs

This one needs regular practice.

Exercise 3: recognizing higher notes

You should not have to work these notes out by counting upwards. Make sure you recognize them instantly.

Exercise 3: the C major scale and arpeggio

Pieces for Lesson 12

When The Saints Go Marching In

Play the section between the repeat bars twice. The first time, play the two bars at the end labeled 1, the second time play the bars labeled 2. These are called *first* and *second time endings*.

Reveille

Military traditional

D.S. al Fine means go back to the sign (𝄋) and play again until *Fine* (end).

Lesson 13 goals:

1. **The note E flat (E♭) in the lower register**
2. **Finger dexterity**

The note E♭ in the lower register

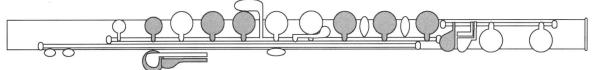

Fast fingers

This is the *don't run before you can walk* bit.

In order to play fast pieces, you must first spend time playing exercises and pieces slowly in order to gain complete control over every muscle that is being used.

Exercise 1:

Practice will help to build up "muscle memory": eventually you won't have to think about which fingers are required for a particular note, as your hands will "know" what to do.

This may seem easy, but aim for a perfect tone and precise finger movement.

Remember the fingering is different for the middle register D and E♭.

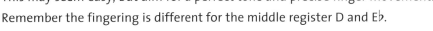

Exercise 2:

Coordinating your fingers can be hard. Be really critical of yourself; if it's not entirely perfect more practice is needed with both of these examples.

Exercise 3:

Play this many times to build up speed.

Pieces for Lesson 13

Camptown Races

Foster

Home On The Range

Pieces for Lesson 13

CD1
69–70

Danny Boy

Irish traditional

This is one of the most beautiful tunes ever written. Spend time on this to ensure complete fluency,
control of dynamics and the correct slurs—it will be time well spent.

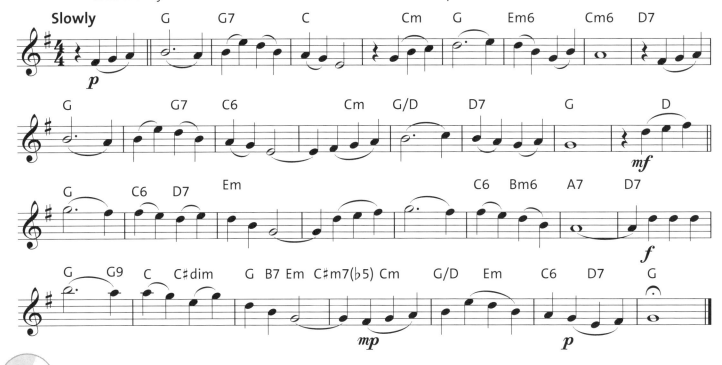

CD1
71

Swing Low, Sweet Chariot

Spiritual

goals:

1. **The note G sharp (G♯)**
2. **Minor keys and scales**

The note G♯

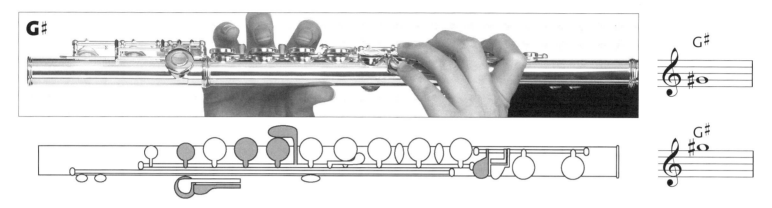

Exercise 1: low G, G♯ and A

This really works your little finger! Look out—the worms of misery are back!

Exercise 2:

The more you practice the G♯, the stronger your little finger will become, so here goes:

Exercise 3:

This is a Scottish folk song: play it vigorously.

Lesson 14

Major and minor

Most of the pieces you have played up to now have sounded cheerful. This is because they are virtually all in a *major* key, C major, F major, G major and so on. Sometimes, however, a composer wishes to express sadness in a piece. In general he or she will do this by writing the piece in a *minor* key.

Exercise 4: the A major scale

Play this a few times and listen to its bright character.

Exercise 5: A minor

The *key signature* is the same as C major, however look out for the G♯s, which are shown as they occur in the music (these are called **accidentals**).

Pieces for Lesson 14

CD1
72–73

Hava Nagila

Israeli traditional

A famous tune in a minor key (Dm). Start slowly and get faster as you go along.
This should sound very exciting!

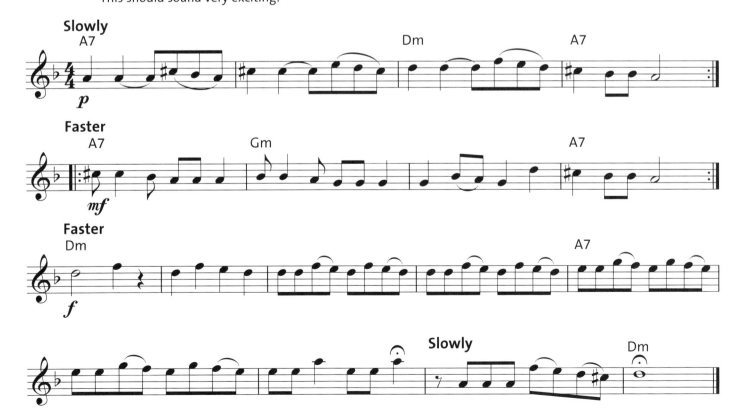

Pieces for Lesson 14

Go Down Moses

Spiritual

The melody is divided up among the three flutes, so they are all equally important.

Use the written dynamics to blend in when you are playing an accompanying line.

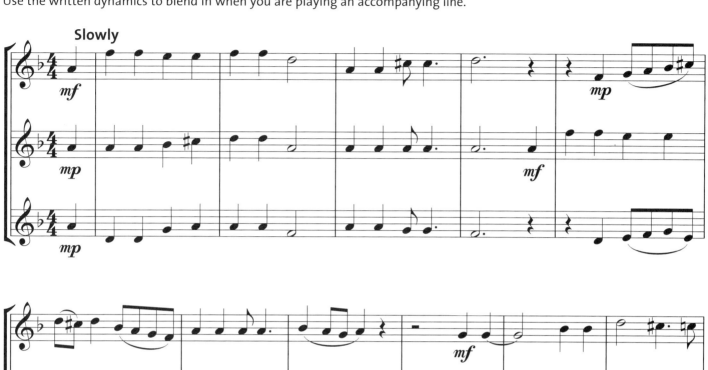

Lesson 15

goals:

1. **The notes C♯ and D in the upper register**
2. **Staccato and legato**

The notes C♯ and D

C♯

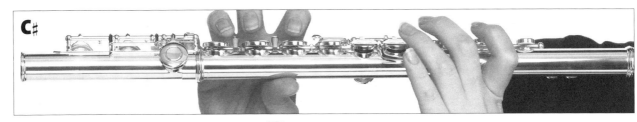

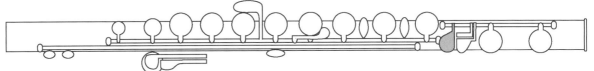

D

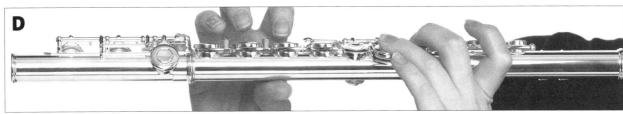

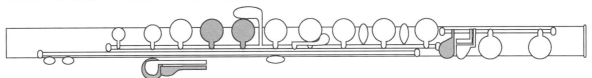

Exercise 1:

Match the tone and volumes of all of these notes.

High notes only use a very short length of the instrument to make a sound. For this reason they need less breath for the same volume than a low note. Be careful not to use too much breath on high notes, otherwise it may affect the tone and the tuning — and your ears!

Exercise 2:

Play smoothly over these notes.

Exercise 3:

This is a two-octave D minor scale.

48

Staccato and legato

Legato means "joined up" and refers to notes that are slurred or tongued smoothly without a gap from the previous one. *Staccato* on the other hand means "detached." This is shown by a dot above or below the note:

Exercise 4:

Repeat this many times to achieve clear staccato tonguing.

Exercise 5:

Begin this very slowly otherwise the eighth notes will be too fast to tongue.

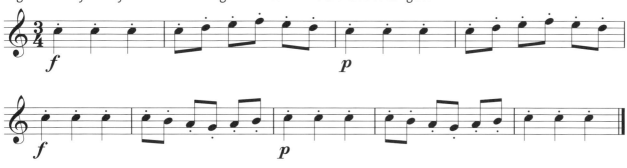

Pieces for Lesson 15

The Blue Danube Waltz

Johann Strauss II

Pieces for Lesson 15

Oh! Susannah

Stephen Foster

Song Of The Volga Boatmen

Russian traditional

Mango Walk

Jamaican traditional

1. Key signatures

On the staff below, draw the correct key signatures for:

G major   F major   D minor   D major   C major

(5)

2. Dots

Simplify the music on the left using dots to get rid of the ties.

(5)

3. Notes

On the staff below draw the following notes as quarter notes:

Low register D and **G♯**, **middle register F♯**, **A**, **C♯**, and **top D**

(6)

4. Dynamics

What do the following words mean?

legato _____

staccato _____

(4)

5. Naming ceremony

Identify all the items indicated by arrows.

(5)

Total **(25)**

1. **The notes C and C♯**
2. **Enharmonic notes**

The notes C and C♯

C

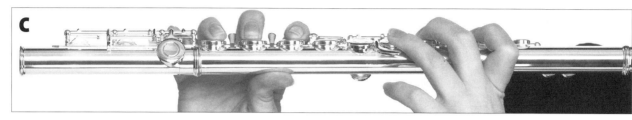

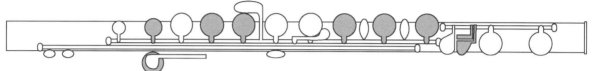

C♯

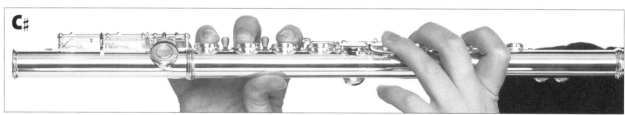

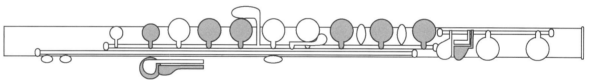

Exercise 1:

Compare the three E♭ notes in different octaves.

Try to keep the tone as similar as possible despite the big difference in pitch. They should all sound as though they are coming from the same instrument.

Play these long notes. Use a full breath for each one.

Don't forget, your little finger is needed for all the notes on a different key each time!

Enharmonic notes

From previous lessons, you know that A♭ is a semitone *below* A, and at the same time a semitone *above* G.

This means that the same note could be called G♯. These two notes are *enharmonic equivalents*.

Exercise 2:

These two short pieces need a note you have already learned, the first as a G♯, the second as an A♭.

Exercise 3:

Play the following notes. You *do* know the fingering for each one, however you may need to write down their enharmonic equivalents first.

G♭/_____?   D♯/_____?   A♯/_____?   D♭/_____?

Pieces for Lesson 16

The Entertainer

Scott Joplin

Enharmonic Blues

Slow blues tempo

Lesson 17 goals:

1. **Gradation of dynamics**
2. **More Italian terms**

Dynamic markings and tempo markings are very useful.

Music should always be expressive, and these markings will give a clue to the way a piece should be played.

All dynamic changes you have played so far have been instant. However, suddenly changing from *piano* to *forte* has a different impact from a gradual change.

Crescendo means gradually get louder, also shown as: ◁──────

Diminuendo means gradually get quieter, also shown as: ▷──────

Some other commonly used Italian words to describe a tempo are:

Allegro quickly   **Andante** at a walking pace   **Adagio** slowly

Rallentando (rall.) becoming slower   **Accelerando** (accel.) becoming faster

Pieces for Lesson 17   *Operatic Duets*

CD1 85

La Forza del Destino   Verdi

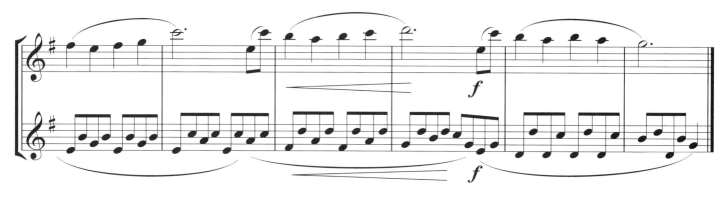

54

Hail The Conquering Hero (from *Judas Maccabeus*)

Handel

William Tell Overture

Rossini

Lesson 18 goals:

1. **Swing eights**
2. **Playing jazz pieces**

Swing

Remember not to play the eighths too "straight," but instead give them a healthy bounce.

You might imagine the beat divided into three, with the first two-thirds for the first eighth and the final third for the second eighth.

In classical music all eighth notes are played exactly as written, that is, lasting half as long as a quarter note. In jazz, however, eighth notes are normally played unevenly, with the first of each pair longer than half a beat, and the second shorter to compensate. This is called **swing**.

Exercise 1:

Play this E minor scale in swing rhythm. Try it first all tongued, then with the slurs as written.

Pieces for Lesson 18

88–89 CD1

Little Brown Jug

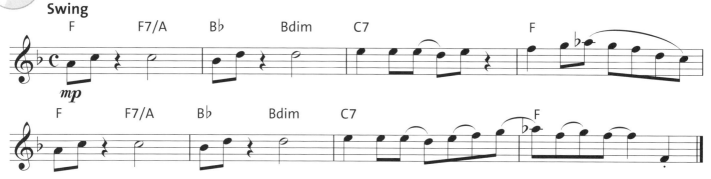

90–91 CD1

Joshua Jazz

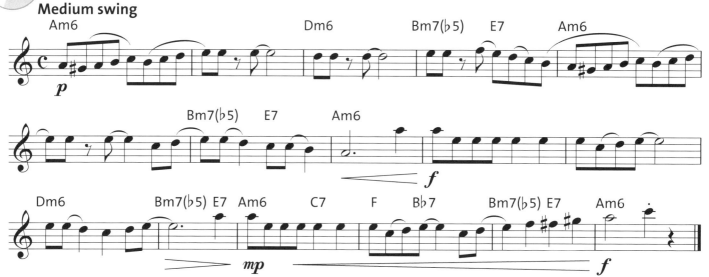

56

Pieces for Lesson 18

Maryland, My Maryland

Moderate swing

Lesson 19

goals:

1. **Good technique through scale practice**
2. **Ensemble playing**

Practicing

Practicing scales every day will help you to:

- Train your fingers to respond quickly in various keys
- Ensure evenness in the timing of notes
- Develop a consistent tone over the instrument's range
- Increase control over your breathing
- Improve your listening awareness of note relationships

The following scales and arpeggios are recommended practice for flautists at a relatively early stage.

They should be practiced both slurred and tongued.

F major

G major

D major (two octaves)

E minor

A minor

Pieces for Lesson 19

Gypsy Rover

Pieces for Lesson 19

Down By The Riverside

Lively swing

goals:

1. $\frac{6}{8}$ time signature (compound time)
2. Traditional-style songs in $\frac{6}{8}$ time

Simple and compound time

$\frac{2}{4}$, $\frac{3}{4}$, and $\frac{4}{4}$ are all *simple* time signatures.

The top number tells you how many beats per bar, and the bottom number tells you that each beat is worth one quarter note. This also means that each beat can be divided into **two** eighth notes.

Exercise 1: counting in simple time

```
Count: 1    2    3    4    1  &  2  &  3  &  4  &    1...
```

In *compound* time, however, each beat is worth **three** eighth notes.

This means that each beat must now be a *dotted* quarter notes.

Exercise 2: counting in compound time

```
Count: 1  &  a  2  &  a    1  &  a  2  &  a    1    2
```

Exercise 3:

Here's a well-known tune in $\frac{6}{8}$ time. Remember to think in *two*.

```
Count: 1  &  a  2  &  a  1  &  a  2  &  a  1  &  a  2  &  a    1...
```

Irish jigs are in $\frac{6}{8}$ time, as is the well-known "We're Off To See The Wizard" from The Wizard Of Oz. $\frac{6}{8}$ pieces are often lively. Counting two groups of three is much easier than trying to count all six eighth notes.

THINK!

Remember to keep a steady beat.
You might want to use a metronome.
Some people like to tap their foot
when they play, but this takes a little
practice before it comes naturally.

Pieces for Lesson 20

The Animals Went In Two By Two

Traditional

For He's A Jolly Good Fellow

Traditional

test: *for* Lessons 16 to 20

1. Enharmonic

Rewrite the following notes as their enharmonic equivalents:

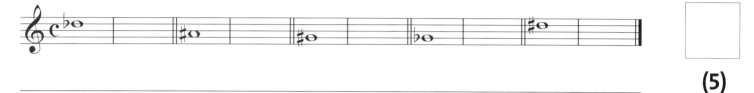

(5)

2. Afraid of heights?

Write the following music one octave higher:

(6)

3. Breath control

Play this note with a steady tone, controlling your breath at all times.

You will score one point (up to a maximum of five) for every three seconds held.

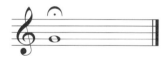

(5)

4. Expression

Write the Italian words for:

Get louder _____   Get quieter _____

Get quicker _____   Get slower _____

(4)

5. Scale test

Play the following from memory:

1. E minor scale

2. D major arpeggio

3. F major scale

4. G major arpeggio

5. A minor scale

(5)

Total **(25)**

Lesson 21 goals:

1. **The note B♭ using the thumb**
2. **Sixteenth notes**

The note B♭ using the thumb key

This is a convenient way of playing B♭ and can be used when playing scales and pieces with flats in the key signature, for example F major, G minor, etc.

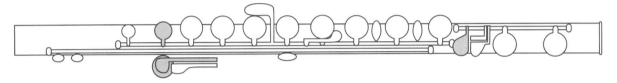

Exercise 1:

Keep your thumb on the B♭ key except when playing C.

Sixteenth notes

You should already be familiar with notes that last four beats (whole note), two beats (half note), one beat (quarter note), and half a beat (eighth note).

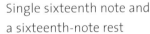

Single sixteenth note and a sixteenth-note rest

Group of four sixteenth notes (worth one quarter note)

One bar of sixteenth notes in 4/4 time

Sixteenth notes last for a *quarter* of the length of a quarter note, or *half* the length of an eighth note.

Exercise 2: Double Or Nothing!

Keep the beat steady and don't start too quickly. Use thumb B♭ here.

Exercise 3: Three beats per bar

Pieces for Lesson 21

Ballad

Ned Bennett

A ballad is a slow jazz piece. Don't *swing* the eighth notes.

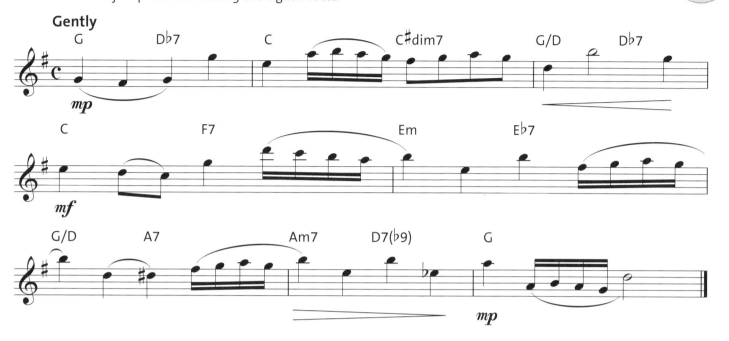

Surprise Symphony (excerpt)

Haydn

The surprise is in the 8th bar of this famous piece. Legend has it that the composer knew that his employer, Count Esterházy, often fell asleep during concerts. The sudden loud note was to wake him up!

Pieces for Lesson 21

Dracula's Dance

Ned Bennett

Sixteenth notes can look scary at first. Practice this very slowly making sure that your half notes, quarter notes, eighth notes, and sixteenth notes are played in tempo.

Allegro

goals:

Lesson 22

1. **The notes high E♭ and high F**
2. **Sixteenth-note groups**

High E♭

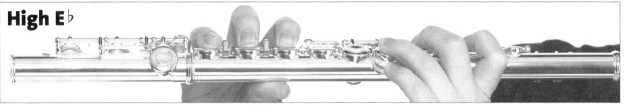

For these notes try aiming the air upwards by pushing your bottom lip slightly forward, and don't rely on blowing too hard.

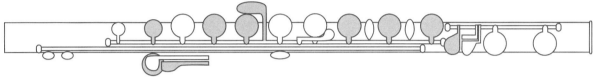 

High F

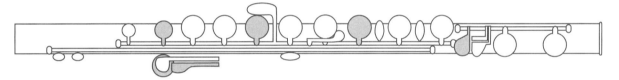 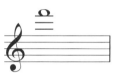

Exercise 1:

E♭ major arpeggio. All E♭s are fingered differently.

F major arpeggio.

In the exercises and pieces of the previous lesson, all the sixteenth notes were in groups of four, lasting a total of one beat. Try to learn these new patterns as rhythmic words rather than trying to count them each time.

Each of these eighth-note and sixteenth-note combinations are grouped into a quarter note's worth of beats.

Exercise 2:

Exercise 3:

Exercise 4:

67

Pieces for Lesson 22

Simple Gifts

Joseph Bracket, Jr.

Frith Street Rag

Ned Bennett

Remember to read the grouped notes as *rhythmic words*.

Moderately

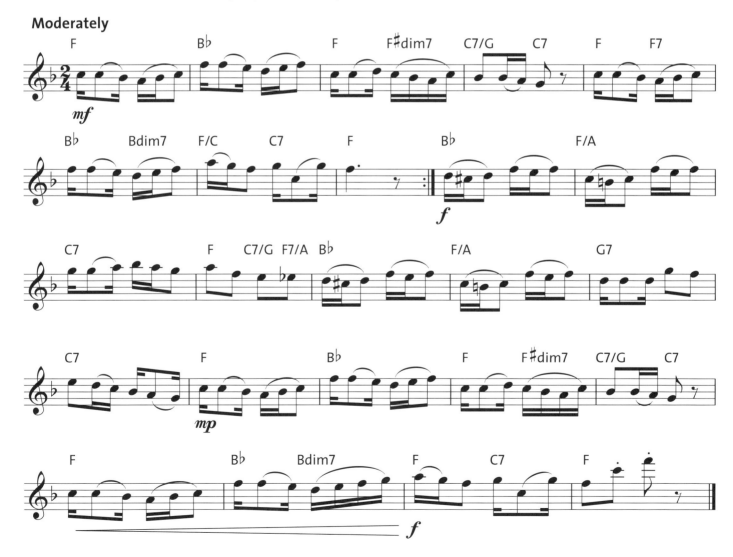

Pieces for Lesson 22

Dance Of The Swans

Tchaikovsky

CD2
10-11

TEMPO TERMS

There are a number of articulation markings in this piece, including staccato, tenuto, and accent markings.

They occur early in the piece, but you must apply the same articulation later on, even if none is marked, in order to achieve a consistent performance.

Allegretto means "a little *Allegro*," being somewhere between **Andante** and **Allegro** in tempo.

Lesson 23

goals:

1. **Dotted pairs**
2. **Scale revision**
3. **Scotch snap**

Dotted pairs

The "dotted pair" is a very common rhythm: a dotted eighth note (worth three sixteenth notes) followed by a sixteenth note. Look at these three examples:

The first note of each pair is three times longer than the second. In the final example, the dotted eighth note is worth 3 sixteenth notes. The final sixteenth note completes the group (worth one quarter note in total).

Exercise 1:

It is very important to keep the 3:1 ratio between the dotted pairs, otherwise they could sound like swing eighth notes which are played in a more relaxed way (more like 2:1).

Exercise 2:

Try playing this entire exercise in tempo. Professional musicians often practice scales in this rhythm as it helps develop coordination between the tongue and the fingers.

The Scotch snap

The Scotch snap is the opposite of the dotted pair.
The sixteenth note comes first, then the dotted eighth note:

Exercise 3:

Here is the scale of E♭ major written in Scotch snap rhythm.

Try this for any of the scales you have learned so far.

Pieces for Lesson 23

Prelude

Chopin

CD2 12

Slowly

mp

mf   *p*

Loch Lomond

Scottish Traditional

CD2 13

Watch out for the Scotch snap rhythms in this one!

Boldly

mf

Pieces for Lesson 23

CD2 14–15

Humoresque

Dvořák

The dotted pairs here are grouped to show each half bar or half note's-worth of beats. Make sure you don't swing this piece. Keep the dotted pairs light and accurate.

goals:

1. **The note high G**
2. **Playing in tune**
3. **Sixteenth notes in 6/8**

High G

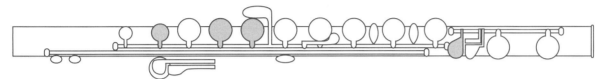

Exercise 1:

Remember to direct the air slightly upwards for the higher notes.

Intonation: playing in tune

In order to play perfectly in tune, a skilled flutist will make very small adjustments to the embouchure to lower or raise notes by minuscule amounts. These adjustments must be automatic otherwise you will have too much to think about when you are playing a piece.

Intonation is the word for tuning individual notes. Good intonation takes a while to achieve. Play this exercise at least three times a week.

Exercise 2:

Make sure you have *warmed up* your flute.

Play a long A (middle octave). Make sure you are perfectly in tune with the piano or CD tuning note.

If you are sharp (too high), pull your headjoint out a little.

Do the opposite if you are flat (too low). Your teacher will be able to guide you.

Now play the following music (in tempo) along with the CD or piano, listening very carefully to every note. If you are in tune, the note will sound pure. If you are sharp, there will be an uncomfortable, grating sound.

To raise (sharpen) the pitch, direct the air upwards using the bottom lip.
To lower (flatten) the pitch direct the air slightly downwards into the hole.

CD2 16

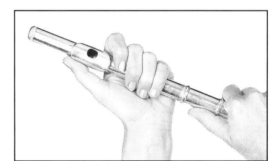

Sixteenth notes in 6/8 time

Below are pairs of sixteenth notes within half a 6/8 bar. As you did with the simple time groups, try to learn these rhythms as words. They have been labeled A to J.

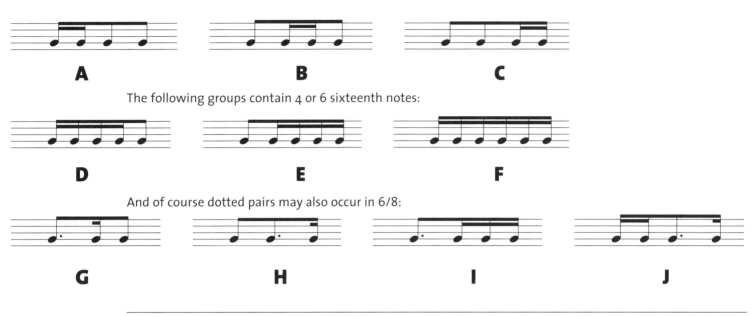

The following groups contain 4 or 6 sixteenth notes:

And of course dotted pairs may also occur in 6/8:

Exercise 2: Combining the groups

Choose a series of 8 groups at random and write it down. Then clap the rhythm that the groups produce.

As each group contains three eighth notes' worth of beats, your piece will be four bars long in 6/8.

Here is an example:

Pieces for Lesson 24

CD2 17

Greensleeves

Attrib. Henry VIII

A well-known melody for practice at playing dotted pairs in 6/8 time. Are you playing the high notes in tune?

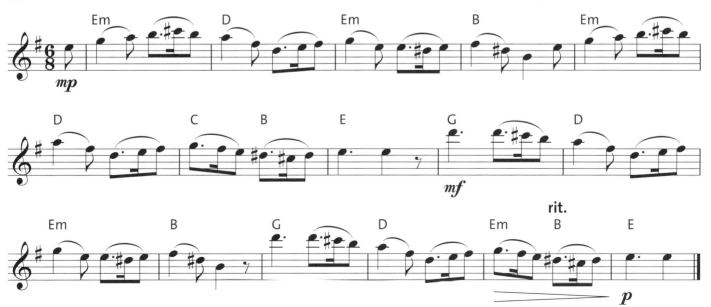

Pieces for Lesson 24

Lillabullero

17th Century

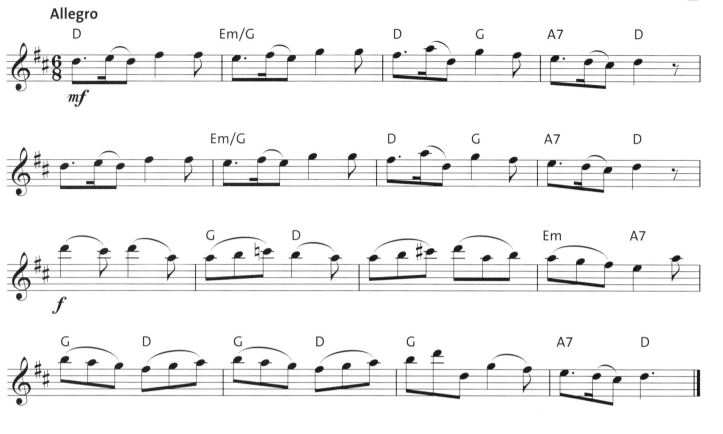

Allegro Moderato

Justano Bardi

Lesson 25 goals:

1. The chromatic scale
2. Good intonation through duet playing

The chromatic scale

Chromatic literally means "colored." The chromatic scale is colored by every note that can be played on your instrument. Each note is one semitone above or below the last one.

Exercise 1:

Play one octave of the chromatic scale starting on F, ascending and descending.
You will find it is best to use the "long" B♭ fingering when needed..

Exercise 2:

Now play the chromatic scale starting on G.

Did you notice that this uses exactly the same notes? You can start and finish the chromatic scale wherever you like, but the notes will always be the same.

Exercise 3:

Here is a chromatic scale to improve your *high* notes. Play the repeated bars many times, slowly at first.
Keep your fingers close to the flute. Don't forget to check your *intonation*.

Exercise 4:

Another chromatic exercise to help improve your *low* notes.
You will need a strong right-hand little finger for this.

Pieces for Lesson 25

When And Where

Ned Bennett

You should learn both parts. Good intonation is vital to make this piece work.

Watch out for chromatic passages.

Slowly

Pieces for Lesson 25

Spring Song

Mendelssohn

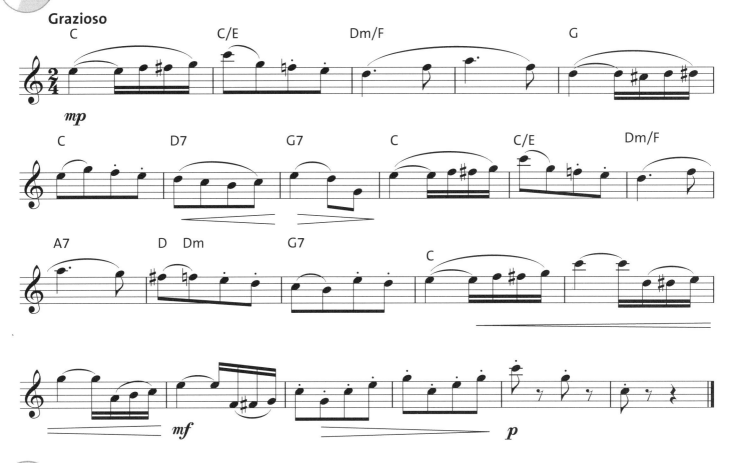

Entry Of The Gladiators

Fučík

First practice this famous tune slowly to work out the notes. Don't lose patience...it's well worth the effort!

goals:

1. The Blues scale
2. Improvisation

The Blues scale

The Blues is a style of music that originated in the American South during the beginning of the 20th century.

Originally a Blues musician would sing while accompanying himself on guitar but, from the 1920s, the Blues was played on piano, saxophone, trumpet, and most jazz instruments.

Most of the melodic content of the Blues uses the Blues scale, a series of notes that gives the music its special character.

Huddie Ledbetter (Leadbelly)

Exercise 1:

There is a Blues scale for every key. Here is the Blues scale in G.

Exercise 2:

Here is a short melody to illustrate how the notes of the Blues scale can sound.
Notice that you can extend the scale above and below the key notes.

Improvisation

One very essential part of Blues (and jazz) is *improvisation*. This means that the musician makes up the melody as he or she goes along. The Blues scale makes this quite easy, as it will fit with all the different chords that accompany the Blues.

Exercise 3:

Make sure you have practiced the G Blues scale so that you can play it without looking.
Play the following four bars. Can't see any notes? Then you'll have to make something up as you go along, but keep the tempo steady!

Pieces for Lesson 26

CD2
26–27

Holy-Moly Blues

Ned Bennett

Play the notated bars as written. Improvise the blank bars using only the notes of the G Blues scale. The slashes indicate the beats in these improvised bars. If you can't think of anything to play, either repeat the notated bar you have just played, or don't play at all…rests are a very important part of all music!

Slow Swing

CD2
28–29

Play This Funky Music

Ned Bennett

Funk is a more modern style than Blues, although it shares many characteristics. Don't swing the eighth notes, and remember to take the *D.C. al Fine* after your improvisation. Sixteen bars may seem like a long time, but it will be over before you know it.

Medium Funk

80

Exercise 4:

Here is the Blues scale in D, ascending and descending over two octaves.

Make sure you can play it fluently and from memory before attempting the next piece.

Alabama Boogie-Woogie

Ned Bennett

**CD2
30**

Traditional Blues uses a 12-bar chord sequence to tie the music together.

This piece follows the 12-bar Blues form. Play the "head" (melody), then two choruses of improvisation, then the head once more, remembering to go to the Coda to finish.

Boogie-Woogie was originally a style of Blues played on the piano. The left hand would play a repeated rhythm throughout that gave the music its driving nature.

81

Lesson 27 goals:

1. **Eighth-note triplets**
2. **The note high E**

Eighth-note triplets

Triplets are a set of three notes that occupy the time that would normally be taken up by two notes of the same value. Look at the following comparison:

Each of the three groups contains notes that add up to one quarter note. Eighth-note triplets (a group of three eighth notes with a "3" written above or below) must be played faster than ordinary eighth notes, but not as fast at sixteenth notes.

Exercise 1:

Play this with a slow and steady beat, putting a slight accent on the notes that coincide with a beat.

Count: *1 2 3 4   1 2 3 4   1   2   3   4   1   2   3   4   1...*

Exercise 2: Eighth notes and eighth-note triplets

It is easy to make the mistake of playing triplets as a group of two sixteenth notes followed by an eighth note. Make sure all three notes are exactly the same length. Try this tongued and slurred as indicated.

The note high E

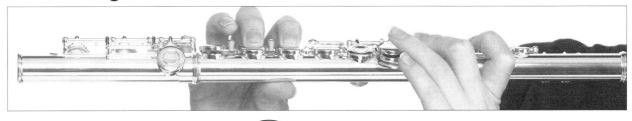

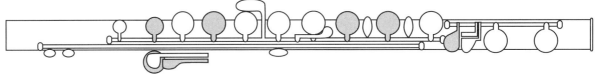

Exercise 3:

The scale and arpeggio of E minor

82

Pieces for Lesson 27

La donna è mobile from Rigoletto

Verdi

Here's a happy tune from a very sad opera. Make sure the dotted pairs are exact.

CD2 31

Barry O'Flynn

Irish Folk Song

CD2 32–33

The instruction "with a swing" actually makes this piece easier. Like jazz, many Irish tunes are written down in the way that's easiest to read.

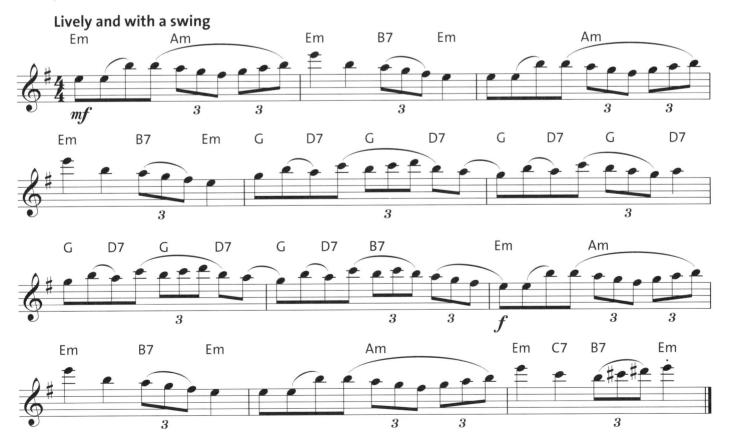

Pieces for Lesson 27

Valse No. 9 (Op. 69, No. 1)

Chopin

Chopin wrote many extremely fast pieces for piano. However, some of his most beautiful music is slow and lyrical. This must be played exactly as written. Although it looks hard, there is a lot of repetition, and remember: *lento* means "slowly," which will help.

goals:

1. Quarter-note triplets
2. Acciaccaturas

Quarter-note triplets

Just as eighth-note triplets occupy the space of two regular eighth notes, a quarter-note triplet fits into the
space of two ordinary quarter notes.

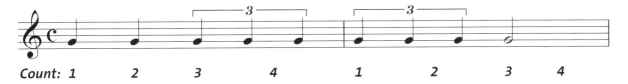

You can see the difficulty here is that while the first note of each group of triplets falls on a beat, the second
and third fall on either side of the next beat.

Exercise 1:

Play both of the following. What do you notice?

Exercise 2:

The accents are there to help you because they always coincide with beats 1 and 3.
Be careful not to play quarter-note triplets as an eighth note-quarter note-eighth note rhythm.

Acciaccatura

This is a very long word for an extremely short note. An acciaccatura (pronounced atch-akka-tour-a) may be
written as a small eighth note or a sixteenth note with a slash through the tail, but should last no time at all
and be slurred to the main note. Whether the acciaccatura comes *just before* the beat or right on it is a topic
of hot debate in classical circles: let your sense of style and phrasing be your guide!

Exercise 3:

Pieces for Lesson 28

CD2
36-37

Triplet Trouble Blues

Ned Bennett

Take this slowly, but still play the acciaccaturas quickly and on the beat, not before.

CD2
38

To The Spring

Edvard Grieg

Listen to the quarter note count-in very carefully. The accompaniment consists of quarter-note triplets, which may make it difficult for you to find the pulse!

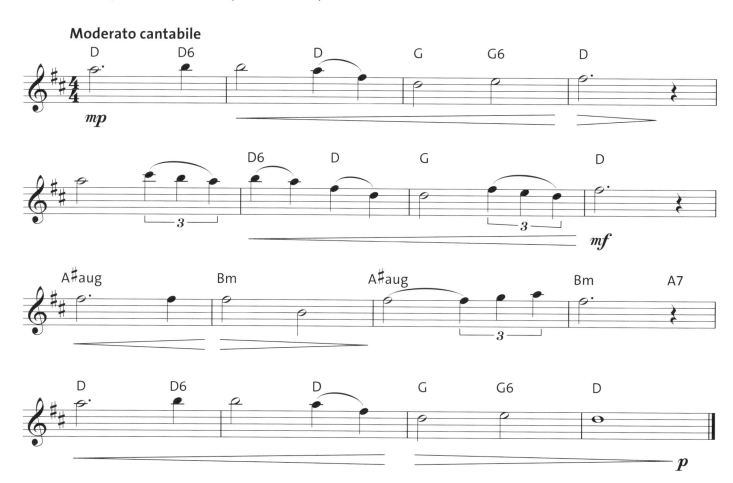

Pieces for Lesson 28

Moment Musical

Schubert

No triplets to worry about here. However, there are plenty of acciaccaturas.

Lesson 29

goals:

1. **Improving your tone**
2. **Breath control**
3. **More dynamics**

Improving your tone

There must have been something about the flute that made you want to learn to play one. When played by an expert, it has a unique sound that can make the hair on the back of your neck stand on end.

Try to record yourself playing one of your favorite pieces from this book. You don't have to hire a recording studio: most computers can record sound, and schools and colleges often have a good recording device.

Listen to the recording. How do you sound compared to your teacher or your favorite flute player on CD? A great tone takes years to develop. It is not just knowing what to do, it is also building up muscles and stamina, just like an athlete would to compete at the highest level.

The following *tone exercises* could be thought of as your flute gym routine.
The more you play these exercises, the better you will sound.

Practice in front of a mirror to check for a relaxed posture, correct embouchure and good hand position. Try to spend five to ten minutes, three times a week, on this routine.

Tone exercise 1:

Breathe in slowly and deeply. Play the first note for a count of 4. Slur to the lower note and hold it for as long as possible using your diaphragm, which will support the sound.

Relax, breathe in slowly, and play the next pair.

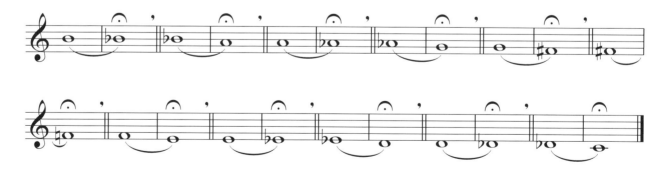

This exercise is to:

- Build muscles so you can keep your throat open and relaxed at all times when playing
- Enlarge your lung capacity and control your airflow using your diaphragm

Tone exercise 2:

Breathe when you need to for this exercise. Play this very slowly but in tempo. Do not get louder the higher you go, and be careful with your intonation. You will need to control the direction of your air very carefully with this exercise.

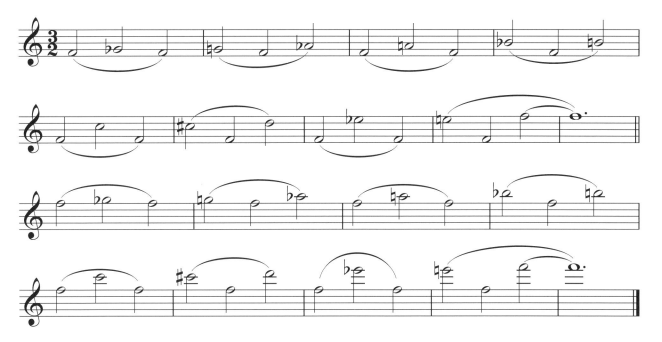

> ### This exercise is to:
>
> - Improve evenness throughout the octaves
> - Increase flexibility and accuracy of embouchure
> - Improve reliability of intonation

Dynamic Extremes

Up till now you have played music with dynamics ranging anywhere from quiet to loud (*p* to *f*).
As your strength and control increases, you could be asked to play very quiet (*pianissimo*) *pp*, or very loud (*fortissimo*) *ff*.

Tone exercise 3:

Breathe in slowly and deeply. Play each note for as long as you can, moving very slowly and smoothly through the dynamics as indicated (as though turning a volume knob). You will need to alter your diaphragm support as well as your embouchure according to the dynamic marking.
Be careful not to go sharp as you get louder.

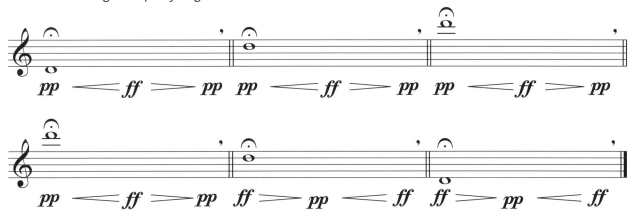

> ### This exercise is to:
>
> - Increase your diaphragm control
> - Improve your intonation
> - Improve awareness of embouchure

Pieces for Lesson 29

Adagietto from Symphony No. 5

Mahler

This should be slow, and very expressive—it ranks among the most passionate music ever written.

goals:

1. The note high F♯
2. Practice routine
3. Trills

High F♯

High F♯

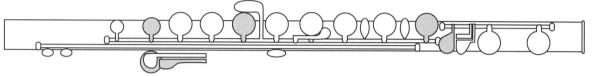

Exercise 1:

High F♯ is a hard note to play. A perfect embouchure is needed for the note to sound.

Practice routine

There is one basic fact that applies to playing every musical instrument: **the more you practice, the quicker you will improve**. Some people enjoy practicing and others don't. However, a fixed daily routine is essential to make the best of your time.

- Try to practice at the same time every day
- Be focused: keep your mind entirely on your practicing
- Remember your goals for the week (new pieces, scales, etc.)

- Spend a good amount of time on technical work; don't just play your favorite pieces
- Don't be impatient: remember that you will only become a better player with practice

Use the following table to log your practice for this week.

Be honest...this is to help *you* work out how to improve at a quicker pace.

Day	Long note warm-ups	Tone *or* Intonation Exercise		Scales	Pieces	Total minutes
		Tone	**Intonation**			

Trills

Although usually found in music from the Baroque era (1600-1750) and the Classical era (1750-1820), trills are a very important form of ornamentation in many styles of music. The written note is rapidly alternated with the note above:

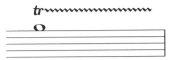

Not exact sixteenth notes, just as fast as possible.

For music written before 1750, begin the trill on the upper note.

Pieces for Lesson 30

Gavotte from Suite No. 3

J. S. Bach (1685-1750)

Look at Bach's dates: on which notes do the trills begin?

Pieces for Lesson 30

Minuetto from Eine Kleine Nachtmusik W. A. Mozart (1756-1791)

This is from the late 18th Century. Play all repeats, then go back to the sign and play to *Fine*, this time without repeating.

Lesson 31 goals:

1. Rubato
2. Solo playing

Rubato

Sometimes, subtly altering the tempo during a piece of music can be very expressive.
Soloists often use a kind of hesitation, or slowing down, to achieve a dramatic effect.
This is known as *rubato* (Italian for "robbed") and is especially effective when used sparingly.

Originally rubato passages "borrowed" time by slowing down, and then caught up with the accompaniment by speeding up later in the phrase. Nowadays playing rubato simply means being flexible with the tempo of the performance to create expression.

Solo playing

A good soloist will know the music by heart. This gives the performer confidence and helps the music to flow much more convincingly.

In most auditions, an unaccompanied piece tests your ability to play *solo*.
You may also be asked to perform in a concert, or you may want to
play for your friends and family.

A guide for solo playing

• If the piece has a lively rhythm, it is essential that you keep the beat steady. Music is a language, and if people can tap their toes to what you are playing, you are communicating with them.

• Never perform a piece so fast that you have to slow down for the tricky passages. Practice everything at one tempo and gradually speed up the whole piece.

• If the piece is dreamier in nature, then allow yourself some rubato. Enjoy the feeling of power that you can control your audience. Make them wait for expressive moments, or increase their excitement by pushing the tempo a little faster.

• Whatever the piece, always think before you play. Try to hear the beginning of the piece in your head... breathe... breathe again... then play.

Solo Pieces for Lesson 31

Sailor's Hornpipe

English Folk Dance

Traditionally this piece begins very slowly and gradually builds up tempo to a fast, rousing conclusion.

However, make sure you can play it all perfectly at a moderate tempo before you try anything fancy.

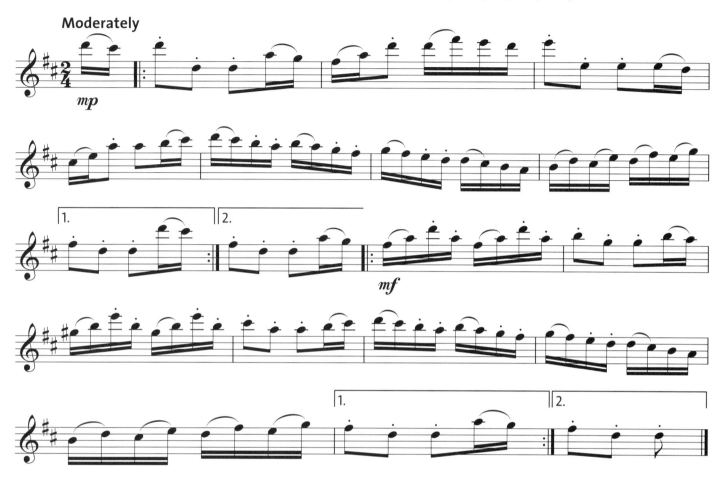

Sometimes I Feel Like A Motherless Child

Spiritual

Here's an opportunity for rubato. Learn the piece keeping to a strict, slow tempo. Then think how you might make it more expressive by changing this at times.

Solo Pieces for Lesson 31

100% Humidity

Ned Bennett

Swing this piece, which uses the G Blues scale. Keep the tempo steady (no rubato), and repeat the improvisation section as many times as you like. You must always relate the notes to the beat which should remain implied by what you play. Take the ideas for your improvisation from the written music if you wish.

Medium Shuffle

goals:

1. **Simple time, compound time, and unusual time signatures**
2. **More scales**

Time signatures

In *simple* time signatures the beat can be divided into two. It means that the music flows predictably and this is why these signatures are the most commonly found:

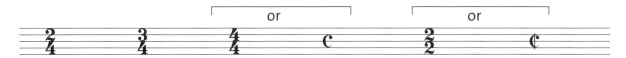

In *compound* time signatures the beat divides into three. The music still flows well.

one beat	two beats	three beats	four beats

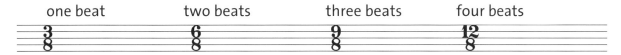

All the pieces that you have played so far in this book use a time signature from the illustrations above. However, many pieces deliberately use a less-flowing time signature:

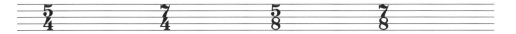

Exercise 1:

Clap the following examples, emphasizing the notes on which accents have been placed.

By the way, the time signature may change at any point in a piece! Have a look at the *Bulgarian Dance* later in this lesson to see an example of this.

Lesson 32

Exercise 2: New scales and arpeggios

G major
two octaves

B minor
a twelfth

Play these according to the time signatures and accents (although normally you should play them with equal weighting for each note).

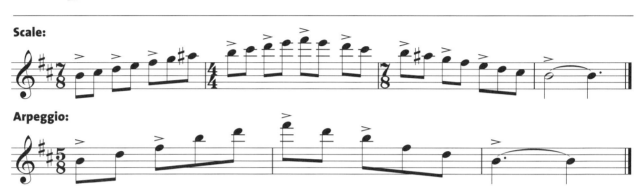

Pieces for Lesson 32

CD2 48–49

Bulgarian Dance

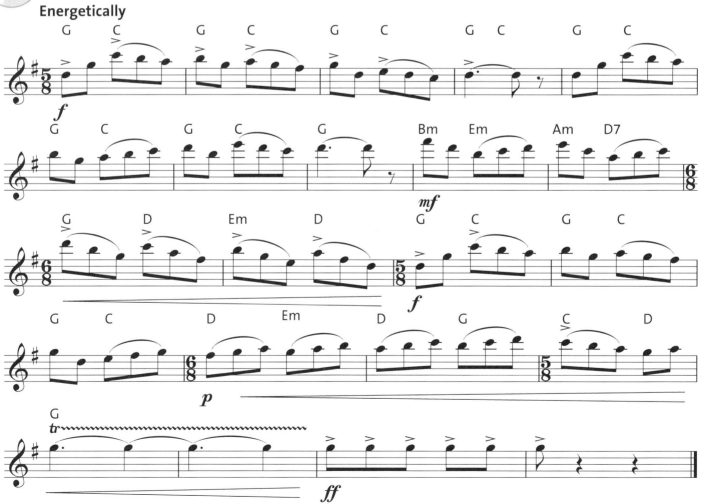

Pieces for Lesson 32

Ut tuo propitiatus

11th Century Organum

At first this piece may sound odd, perhaps rather modern and experimental, even though it was written almost a thousand years ago. Try to find a church or large hall with lots of reverberation in which to play it. Originally this would have been sung by monks. However, the sound of two flutes can be equally as haunting.

Don't play this fast, and stick to a strict tempo until the very end.

Dexterity

You may have listened to a piece of music that is so fast you can hardly hear the individual notes.
When played well, this can sound impressive and exciting. However, it takes a long time and endless patience to develop the skill needed to play very quickly.

Exercise 1:

Practice these exercises regularly, instead of (or in addition to) your intonation and tone exercises.

This exercise uses patterns of the first three notes of every major scale. Make sure you spend more time with the patterns you can't play very well in order to play the whole exercise at a reasonable tempo, both slurred and tongued (which is hard!).

The first key has been written out in full. Play the rest in the same manner.

Exercise 2:

This one is chromatic and happens to work down through the keys, but you could equally work up.
Follow the articulation carefully (slurs, tongued notes, and staccatos), keeping the sound as clean as you can.

Pieces for Lesson 33

Caprice No. 24 (theme)

Paganini

Presto means fast. This piece was originally written for violin, but it has been arranged for piano, cello, and jazz band as well as flute.

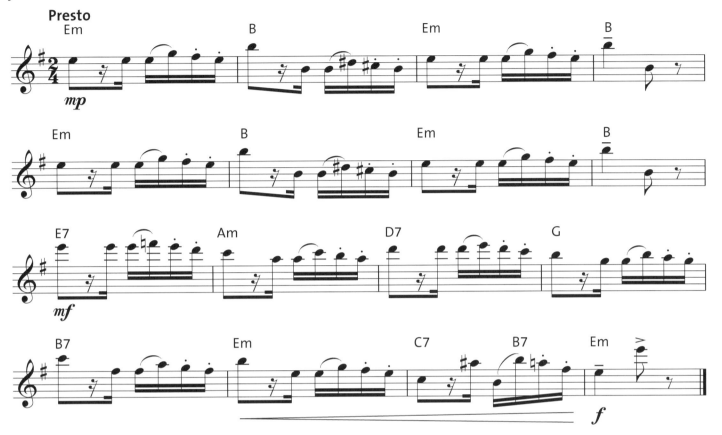

The Irish Washer Woman

Irish 18th Century

Coordination between your tongue and fingers is essential for this piece.

Pieces for Lesson 33

Czardas

Monti

Play the first (slow) section with just a little rubato. The second section needs to be very fast.

As with all fast music, practice it slowly but in tempo otherwise you will never learn the correct timing.

goals:

1. Endurance
2. Sensitivity

Playing for any length of time puts a strain on certain muscles. Think of running an 800 meter race. The first lap is usually okay, but you will feel the pain in your legs during the second lap. This is because when you tighten your muscles, blood cannot flow through them. Your embouchure muscles go through the same process in a long piece.

It is important to keep your entire body relaxed when you play.

Don't forget to be sensitive to the other musicians. In this piece you will sometimes have an interesting melody, but sometimes you will be accompanying other players. Adjust your dynamic level (volume) to reflect this during this 16th century masterpiece.

Alla riva del Tebro (madrigal)
Palestrina

Although the notes in this quartet seem easy, playing it will be hard. Make sure you count like crazy.
If you get lost you will find it almost impossible to find your place again.

1. Concert Performance

Concert Performance

Having worked through books 1 and 2 of *A New Tune A Day*, you should be ready to perform as part of a concert, whether for friends and family, at school, or for an audience you've never met.

> Give yourself the best chance of success with these golden rules.
>
> **1. Know your music.**
> You must be able to play all your pieces, perfectly and without thinking. Musicians play much better if they have memorized the music.
>
> **2. Look the part.**
> Dress professionally and present yourself as you would for meeting someone very important. This will help you to feel confident when you play.
>
> **3. Breathe slowly and deeply before you play.**
> This will help overcome nerves and oxygenate your brain, helping you to concentrate. It also lets you pause to think about the piece.
>
> **4. Bow slowly to the audience when they clap.**
> This is good manners, as if to say "thank you for listening to me."

Pieces for Lesson 35

The following pieces are all great for a performance. Even if you are playing them just for practice or fun, imagine you are giving a live performance and play with all the expression, technique, and accuracy you can.

CD2 54–55

Wedding Dance

Kazakhstan

Here is a fiddly melody with many complications, but rewarding to play if you practice it carefully.

Energetic
E and B ped. accomp.

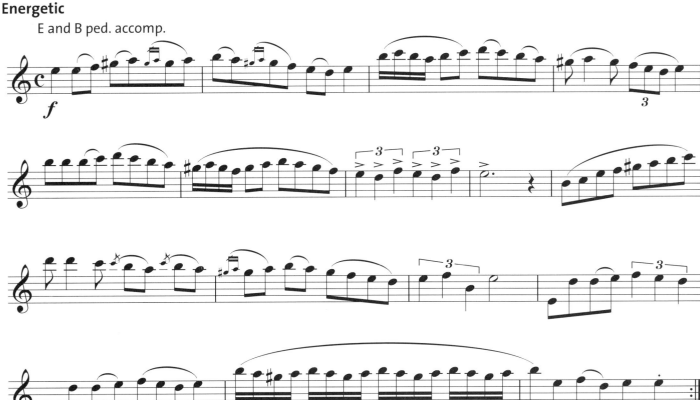

Pieces for Lesson 35

Waltz from Die Fledermaus

Strauss

This is a fine, flowing waltz that needs lots of energy to perform.

This piece is always performed as part of the New Year's Day concert in Vienna, Austria.

Oh, Won't You Sit Down

Spiritual

This piece has been arranged in a jazz style. Play swing eighth notes, and instead of the written notes, play a D Blues scale improvisation in the section marked *solo ad lib* if you prefer.

Pieces for Lesson 35

Hungarian Dance No. 5

Brahms

Finally, an exciting romp to finish the book. Watch out for the tempo changes towards the end, and make sure your fingers know the notes by themselves.

CD 1: backing tracks

1   Tuning track
2   Virtuoso Performance
3   Valley Song
4   Going Cuckoo
5   Au Clair de la Lune *demonstration*
6   Au Clair de la Lune *backing only*
7   Back To Bed *demonstration*
8   Back To Bed *backing only*
9   Grumpy Graham
10 Medieval Dance
11 Barcarolle
12 Jingle Bells *demonstration*
13 Jingle Bells *backing only*
14 Largo from New World Symphony *demonstration*
15 Largo from New World Symphony *backing only*
16 Lightly Row
17 Knight Time *demonstration*
18 Knight Time *backing only*
19 When The Saints Go Marching In *demonstration*
20 When The Saints Go Marching In *backing only*
21 Joshua Fought The Battle Of Jericho *demonstration*
22 Joshua Fought The Battle Of Jericho *backing only*
23 Coventry Carol *demonstration*
24 Coventry Carol *backing only*
25 Barcarolle
26 Abide With Me
27 Juggling *demonstration*
28 Juggling *backing only*
29 My Favorite Waltz *demonstration*
30 My Favorite Waltz *backing only*
31 Minuet *demonstration*
32 Minuet *backing only*
33 Steal Away *demonstration*
34 Steal Away *backing only*
35 Sea Song
36 Finger Blues *demonstration*

37 Finger Blues *backing only*
38 O Come All Ye Faithful *demonstration*
39 O Come All Ye Faithful *backing only*
40 Skye Boat Song *demonstration*
41 Skye Boat Song *backing only*
42 Scarborough Fair
43 Yankee Doodle *demonstration*
44 Yankee Doodle *backing only*
45 Can Can *demonstration*
46 Can Can *backing only*
47 Nessun Dorma *demonstration*
48 Nessun Dorma *backing only*
49 Magic Flute *demonstration*
50 Magic Flute *backing only*
51 Swing Low, Sweet Chariot *demonstration*
52 Swing Low, Sweet Chariot *backing only*
53 Auld Lang Syne *demonstration*
54 Auld Lang Syne *backing only*
55 Allegro from *Spring*
56 Hark! The Herald Angels Sing *demonstration*
57 Hark! The Herald Angels Sing *backing only*
58 Dixie *demonstration*
59 Dixie *backing only*
60 from *Symphony No. 9*
61 Romance No.1 *demonstration*
62 Romance No.1 *backing only*
63 Can Can *demonstration*
64 Can Can *backing only*
65 When The Saints Go Marching In
66 Camptown Races
67 Home On The Range *demonstration*
68 Home On The Range *backing only*
69 Danny Boy *demonstration*
70 Danny Boy *backing only*
71 Swing Low, Sweet Chariot
72 Hava Nagila *demonstration*

73 Hava Nagila *backing only*
74 The Blue Danube *demonstration*
75 The Blue Danube *backing only*
76 Oh! Susannah *demonstration*
77 Oh! Susannah *backing only*
78 Song Of The Volga Boatmen *demonstration*
79 Song Of The Volga Boatmen *backing only*
80 Mango Walk *demonstration*
81 Mango Walk *backing only*
82 The Entertainer
83 Enharmonic Blues *demonstration*
84 Enharmonic Blues *backing only*
85 La Forza del Destino
86 Hail The Conquering Hero
87 William Tell Overture
88 Little Brown Jug *demonstration*
89 Little Brown Jug *backing only*
90 Joshua Jazz *demonstration*
91 Joshua Jazz *backing only*
92 Maryland, My Maryland
93 The Animals Went In Two By Two
94 For He's A Jolly Good Fellow *demonstration*
95 For He's A Jolly Good Fellow *backing only*

How to use the CD

The tuning note on track 1 is an A.

After track 2, which gives an idea of how the flute can sound, the backing tracks are listed in the order in which they appear in the book. Look for the symbol in the book for the relevant backing track.

Where both parts of a duet are included on the CD, the top part is in one channel and the bottom part is in the other channel.

CD 2: backing tracks

1   Tuning Note   A
2   Ballad *demonstration*
3   Ballad *backing only*
4   Surprise Symphony (Haydn) *backing only*
5   Dracula's Dance *demonstration*
6   Dracula's Dance *backing only*
7   Simple Gifts *backing only*
8   Frith Street Rag *demonstration*
9   Frith Street Rag *backing only*
10   Dance Of The Swans (Tchaikovsky) *demonstration*
11   Dance Of The Swans (Tchaikovsky) *backing only*
12   Prelude (Chopin) *backing only*
13   Loch Lomond *backing only*
14   Humoresque (Dvořák) *demonstration*
15   Humoresque (Dvořák) *backing only*
16   Exercise 2 (Lesson 24) *backing only*
17   Greensleeves *backing only*
18   Lillabullero *demonstration*
19   Lillabullero *backing only*
20   Allegro Moderato (Bardi) *demonstration*
21   Allegro Moderato (Bardi) *backing only*
22   Spring Song (Mendelssohn) *demonstration*
23   Spring Song (Mendelssohn) *backing only*
24   Entry Of The Gladiators (Fučík) *demonstration*
25   Entry Of The Gladiators (Fučík) *backing only*
26   Holy-Moly Blues *demonstration*
27   Holy-Moly Blues *backing only*
28   Play This Funky Music *demonstration*
29   Play This Funky Music *backing only*
30   Alabama Boogie-Woogie *backing only*

31   La donna è mobile (Verdi) *backing only*
32   Barry O'Flynn *demonstration*
33   Barry O'Flynn *backing only*
34   Valse No. 9 (Chopin) *demonstration*
35   Valse No. 9 (Chopin) *backing only*
36   Triplet Trouble Blues *demonstration*
37   Triplet Trouble Blues *backing only*
38   To The Spring (Grieg) *backing only*
39   Moment Musical (Schubert) *demonstration*
40   Moment Musical (Schubert) *backing only*
41   Adagietto from Symphony No. 5 (Mahler) *backing only*
42   Gavotte from Suite No. 3 (Bach) *demonstration*
43   Gavotte from Suite No. 3 (Bach) *backing only*
44   Minuetto (Mozart) *demonstration*
45   Minuetto (Mozart) *backing only*
46   Sometimes I Feel Like A Motherless Child *demonstration*
47   100% Humidity *demonstration*
48   Bulgarian Dance *demonstration*
49   Bulgarian Dance *backing only*
50   Caprice No. 24 (Paganini) *backing only*
51   The Irish Washer Woman *backing only*
52   Czardas (Monti) *demonstration*
53   Czardas (Monti) *backing only*
54   Wedding Dance *demonstration*
55   Wedding Dance *backing only*
56   Waltz from Die Fledermaus (Strauss) *demonstration*
57   Waltz from Die Fledermaus (Strauss) *backing only*
58   Oh, Won't You Sit Down *demonstration*
59   Oh, Won't You Sit Down *backing only*

60   Hungarian Dance No. 5 (Brahms) *demonstration*
61   Hungarian Dance No. 5 (Brahms) *backing only*